"*Praise to the Man*"

Fifteen Classic BYU Devotionals

about the Prophet Joseph Smith

1955–2005

Order from
Speeches
218 UPB
Brigham Young University
Provo, UT 84602
http://speeches.byu.edu

PRINTED IN THE UNITED STATES OF AMERICA

CONTENTS

Parallel Prophets: Paul and Joseph Smith

Richard Lloyd Anderson

W here is the clear voice of authority on right and wrong? Divided and drifting churches supply religious philosophers but not prophets. Yet Latter-day Saints testify that Joseph Smith and his successors were called to rescue a world adrift in its own conceits and problems. Such a claim can be tested by the Bible, the record of prior prophets.

Would you assist me in making an important point? I would like to report accurately your awareness of the Bible, but remember that the value of the result depends upon your strict honesty now. I have two simple questions. First, do you know who delivered the Sermon on the Mount? If you do, raise your hand. Second, could you name all four Gospels in the New Testament? If you can, raise your hand. We have here observed that an audience of Latter-day Saints college students can score nearly 100 percent in a simple literacy test about Christ. A Gallup poll this year determined that only 42 percent of Americans could name Jesus as delivering the Sermon on the Mount; only 59 percent of the college graduates in this country knew who

Richard Lloyd Anderson was a professor of religion at BYU when this devotional address was given on 9 August 1983. © Brigham Young University.

gave the sermon. Obviously a lower percentage know the critical teachings of that sermon. The national results on your second question are similar. Whereas about 85 percent of you indicated that you could name the four Gospels, only 46 percent of Americans can do so; again, only 61 percent of college graduates can name the four Gospels.[1]

There could not be a stronger argument for a college education of the kind that you are getting, blending scriptural and secular knowledge. This world cannot rise higher than nominal Christianity until the message of Christ and his prophets is learned by educated people. Another name for religious education is missionary work. We must share our reasons for Joseph Smith as a modern prophet, restoring the religious insights to bring all to Christ in this world and in eternity.

As a religion teacher who taught many of your parents, I wish to share an approach to Joseph Smith that grows naturally out of an informed view of the Bible. I have spent half of my time studying the sources of the life of Joseph Smith, and the other half studying the words of Christ and the New Testament prophets. I find it hard to believe in the biblical prophets without also accepting Joseph Smith and those called after him. The same reasons that lead a thinking person to accept Peter and Paul as Christ's servants should also lead that person to accept Joseph Smith as commissioned by Christ. Here I am going to take Paul as an example because we know more about his life than that of any other New Testament prophet. His main strengths as a prophet are also those of Joseph Smith. If you forget some comparisons, please remember the principle—that the leading evidences that Paul is a true prophet also support Joseph Smith as called of God. Remembering that fundamental proposition, you can reconstruct this talk anytime with you own examples. Proof of the mission of any true prophet gives the format for identifying a later true prophet.

PAUL AND JOSEPH SMITH DIFFERENT

This approach does not assume that any individual is a carbon copy of another. Paul was not striking in person whereas Joseph Smith impressed most visitors by his height and bearing. Paul was a missionary apostle whereas Joseph Smith presided over apostles and mostly directed missionary work instead of traveling to do it personally. Paul had the best education that his culture could afford whereas Joseph Smith was raised in frontier poverty without training beyond junior high school skills. But in spite of such wide personal differences, there are dramatic common denominators. It matters little that one spoke English and that the other was fluent in Hebrew and Greek, provided they both spoke as inspired by the Holy Ghost. It is the question of their common calling and authority and revelation that we are addressing. This forces us to go behind appearances to inner spiritual realities. In doing this with Paul and Joseph Smith, we may also increase our abilities to be sensitive to the inner spiritual realities of those prophets who lead and will lead us in our own lives.

PAUL AND JOSEPH HAD DIRECT REVELATION

Both Paul and Joseph Smith were considered blasphemers by their contemporaries. Their sin? They had added to the traditional scriptures. Paul was considered anti-Jewish, and followers of Joseph Smith today are superficially labeled as non-Christian. But every Jewish and Christian prophet had added to the prior revelations by speaking God's message for a new generation. Paul demonstrated this continuity by standing before the Jewish high council and observing that he was on trial for believing what other Pharisees believed—the reality of the resurrection (see Acts 23:6). And Joseph Smith made the same kind of plea in a letter testifying to his nonmember uncle, who later joined the Church. He contended that the revelations to earlier servants of God were the history of religion, not religion. True religion demanded present communication with God. The great answers of God to biblical leaders were really an invitation to seek those answers anew. Joseph Smith asked his uncle, "And have I not an equal privilege with the ancient Saints? And will not the Lord hear my prayers, and listen to my cries as soon as he ever did to theirs, if I come to him in the manner they did?"[2] No true servant of God teaches that the day of continuing revelation is past.

The following story about Joseph Smith comes from Parley P. Pratt's autobiography, a fast-moving introduction to Church history that is a must in your gospel education. Parley P. Pratt was in Philadelphia in January 1840, when Joseph Smith spoke at a meeting during the Christmas recess of Congress, before which he had testified on behalf of Latter-day Saint reparations after the Missouri persecutions. Joseph's counselor, the eloquent Sidney Rigdon, spoke at length on biblical evidences for the Restoration. But Joseph virtually sprang to the pulpit afterward to tell his personal experiences of how God called him, "bearing testimony of the visions he had seen, the ministering angels which he had enjoyed."[3] When Paul was challenged on the resurrection, he did not argue with the Corinthians about the philosophical possibility. On the contrary, he answered their objections only after insisting that he and others knew for themselves, for they had seen. If there is no resurrection, "we are found false witnesses of God" (1 Corinthians 15:15). The essential job of a prophet is to testify personally. And in the case of the great prophets Paul and Joseph Smith, they did so on the basis of their eyewitness contact with Christ.

THEIR FIRST VISIONS

Thus there was a "first vision" for both Paul and Joseph Smith. Their backgrounds differed, but the vision near Damascus and the vision in the New York forest were orientations for these two prophets for a lifetime of service. Both open revelations told them to change their course and to wait for the Lord's further instruction. And both were conversations with the resurrected Christ. Criticisms of Joseph Smith demand consistency in studying the prophets. Many Christians accepting Paul comfortably think that their sniping at Joseph Smith's first vision has proved it wrong. But what appears is a double standard for these critics. Most arguments against Joseph Smith's first vision detract from Paul's Damascus experience with equal force. For instance, Joseph's credibility is attacked because he did not describe his first vision until a dozen years after it happened. But the first known mention of the Damascus appearance is in 1 Corinthians 9:1, written about two dozen years after it happened. Critics love to dwell on supposed inconsistencies in Joseph Smith's spontaneous accounts of his first vision. But people normally give shorter and longer accounts of a vivid experience that is retold more than once. Joseph Smith was cautious about public explanations of his sacred experiences until the Church grew strong and could properly publicize what God had given him. Thus his most detailed first-vision account came after several others—at the time that he began his formal history that he saw as one of the key responsibilities of his life (see JS-H 1:1–2, 17–20). In Paul's case there is the parallel. His most detailed account of Christ's call is the last recorded mention of several. Thus before Agrippa, Paul related how the glorified Savior first prophesied his work among the gentiles; this was told only then because Paul was speaking before a gentile audience (see Acts 26:16–18). Paul and Joseph Smith had reasons for delaying full details of their visions until the proper time and place.

The first visions of Paul and Joseph Smith underline the directness of their divine contact. Many writers now use *prophet* of religious leaders who are eloquent but do not merit that designation. But the overused *awesome* correctly pictures Joseph Smith and Paul standing in the presence of the resurrected Lord and receiving specific direction. Yet such powerful visions did not happen every day. Divine beings do not appear to anyone because of easy whim or casual desire. Such great revelations come when God has a purpose for them. In Paul's case, he saw the Lord on four other known occasions after his first vision—stretching through the next twenty-five years of his career in the Church.[4] Joseph Smith is very similar in the number of other times he saw the Lord throughout seventeen years after his first vision.[5] Neither Paul nor Joseph Smith fell into the impostor's trap of overclaiming such sacred experiences. And there is a corollary here that is a mark of true prophets. Visions supplement agency— they do not supplant it. For years Paul struggled in a lesser light and even opposed the truth before his first vision. We know that Joseph Smith also had a history of years of inquiry. Great answers come after intense quests. Every vision of Joseph Smith or Paul represents an important answer at a critical time.

OUR INVOLVEMENT

Each of us here is involved in the deepest realities given to these great prophets. For one thing, their visions tell us of our personal destinies. Nothing is more religiously exciting than the brilliant scene of three degrees of glory in Joseph Smith's vision recorded in Doctrine and Covenants, section 76. One proof of his inspiration is that the Christian world knows nothing of such degrees of glory—only the superficial heaven or the dismal hell. Yet Paul spoke of himself in humility as "a man in Christ" who was caught up to the "third heaven" to see glorious things (see 2 Corinthians 12:2–4). Joseph Smith and Paul agree here against the Christian world because they received true revelation that religious leaders do not have. In the modern Prophet's words, "When any person receives a vision of heaven, he sees things that he never thought of before."[6] Our origin and destiny are among the most powerful appeals of the restored gospel, and both are vivid in Paul.

There is another dimension where we may identify personally with the prophets. Though they were given great doctrinal guidelines to share, they did not know all answers to everything. Several statements of Joseph Smith regarding judgments and the Second Coming mirror this 1839 comment, "I know not how soon these things will take place."[7] Paul could shatter the arrogance of the Corinthians by comparing human knowledge to the understanding of a child: "for we know in part, and we prophesy in part" (1 Corinthians 13:9). The revealed part is critical for our perspective on earth, but the unrevealed part is essential to our agency and growth in learning through discernment and consistency with revelation.

And just at this point is one of the greatest personal messages from these prophets—the invitation for all to become prophets. The sharp distinction between the clergy and the common man never existed when prophets were on the earth. From the point of view of authority and doctrinal revelation, the New Testament apostles clearly had a special position of leadership. But from the point of view of sharing God's inspiration, they invited all to be baptized, receive the Holy Ghost by the laying on of hands, and participate in the gifts of the Spirit. While correcting excesses, Paul encouraged the early Saints to "desire spiritual gifts" and seek to "prophesy" (1 Corinthians 14:1). Joseph Smith's similar invitation comes in many forms but permeates his speeches. It proves that true prophets do not seek to maintain professional status in an exclusive group, but to lead all to the same power that God has shared with them. On a half-dozen occasions Joseph Smith affirmed that he claimed to be a prophet but added, in the words of Revelation 19:10, that everyone else who could gain a testimony of Jesus would also be a prophet, "for the testimony of Jesus is the spirit of prophecy."[8] That is, if all pay the price to gain the Holy Ghost, all can be prophets. The parallel between Joseph Smith and Paul is vivid here, for Paul penned the most impressive perspective of the Holy Ghost: "the things of God" can only be revealed "unto us by his Spirit"—that which searches "the deep things of God" (1 Corinthians 2:9–11). In turn Joseph Smith gave the most practical advice on how to identify these subtle but powerful spiritual promptings. "A person may profit by noticing the first intimation of the spirit of revelation," Joseph Smith counseled. Proceeding, he asked you to pay attention "when you feel pure intelligence flowing unto you—it may give you sudden strokes of ideas."[9]

Is anyone here not concerned with a relationship with God? Paul and Joseph Smith are trustworthy guides. Their spiritual qualities stand out as impressively similar. Paul's mature letters refer to constant prayers for the Saints, and his hope that they will pray for him. The great miracle of being freed from prison by an earthquake came in the midst of the prayers of Paul and his companion (see Acts 16:25). Joseph Smith's pattern is better documented, not only in his early prayers before his early visitations. Joseph Smith's many letters, personal diaries, and Nauvoo speeches are interspersed with open prayers for the blessings of God upon his work and upon the Latter-day Saints in that work. These are not staged references, but the spontaneous appeals of a sincere man. We are trusting in God's answers to men who deeply trusted him.

THEIR AUTHORITY

And their authority in representing God is overwhelming—they knew that they knew. Paul answered when challenged, "Am I not an apostle? . . . Have I not seen Jesus Christ our Lord?" (1 Corinthians 9:1). Public and private remarks of Paul and Joseph Smith are filled with the personal knowledge of their authority to speak for Jesus Christ. That needs no demonstration in the case of the ancient apostle, who constantly preached Christ to a world that had scarcely heard of him. Since Joseph Smith was sent centuries later to a society that professed belief in Christ, he did not argue that point as much as explain the meaning of Christ's will. Yet his closeness to the Lord is symbolized by his private letters to his wife, which were dashed off with no thought of publication. In 1832 he told her of delay in returning home, mentioned his heartfelt prayers to God for forgiveness and blessings, and spoke of God as his friend and comfort, continuing: "I have given my life into his hands. I am prepared to go at his call. I desire to be with Christ. I count not my life dear to me, only to do his will."[10] Joseph Smith was a powerful witness of Christ not only in the first vision, but in the visions of the three degrees of glory and in the Savior's appearance to accept the Kirtland Temple. But strangely, the followers of this prophet who knew Christ personally are slandered as not Christians by their detractors. Joseph Smith and Paul furnish the most powerful testimonies of Christ outside the records of his ministry.

THEIR TEACHINGS OF SACRIFICE FOR THE GOSPEL

That raises the central issue of Christ's religion. Can one become a Christian through words alone? Isn't it odd that the saved-by-grace tracts seldom quote Christ and his central Sermon on the Mount? If Paul taught salvation by grace alone or faith alone, that would be a major cleavage from Joseph Smith, but it is not. Let's start with the foundation of the Savior whom both served. Jesus closed the

Sermon on the Mount with the warning that hearing (or reading) these sayings without doing them would produce a moral catastrophe similar to the house that collapsed because it was not built on a sound foundation. In half a dozen letters Paul listed the moral sins that will keep one from God's kingdom if not repented of, saying to the Galatians, "I tell you before, as I have also told you in time past, that they which do such things shall not inherit the kingdom of God" (Galatians 5:21). What could be better proof of apostasy than the change of the Christian religion from a religion of action to a religion of belief alone? Newspaper stories of business fraud or repulsive immoralities are reminders that no Latter-day Saint goes into God's kingdom because of his name—only because of his repentance and high performance after accepting Christ's atonement.

Joseph Smith taught a restored gospel filled with mercy and the love of the Savior. But he consistently added the principle of responsibility after learning of mercy. There is no such thing as easy salvation. Someone once said of education: "Never say that learning is fun. It is difficult, painful, hard work. But it is worth it." You who have just about finished a successful semester knew the satisfaction of progress based on discipline. And Joseph Smith consistently taught salvation based on successfully controlling one's body for good. Thus salvation is not easy and pleasurable. But paying the price is worth the magnificent reward. Like Paul, Joseph Smith taught that unrepentant evil would not be ignored on the day of judgment. At a funeral he appealed to all to put their lives in order now: "Let it prove as a warning to all men to deal justly before God with all men—then we shall be clean in the day of judgment."[11] Paul taught accountability throughout his letters, and throughout his Nauvoo preaching Joseph Smith insisted that eternal judgment was among the first principles of the gospel.[12] Indeed, how to meet that judgment successfully is the gospel.

One night's binge on TV or $20 spent on movie tickets would be enough to prove that the motivating principle of this world is pleasure. But the motivating principle of Paul and Joseph Smith was putting aside easy pleasure to bring about God's kingdom. When the Corinthians doubted the resurrection, Paul simply asked why he risked his life "every hour" and faced death "daily" (1 Corinthians 15:30). Would one of Paul's intelligence live a life of discomfort for something not true? To his Corinthian detractors, he simply asked who had given more for the gospel. Paul's record is magnificent in a simple modern translation:

> *From the Jews five times I received forty stripes minus one. Three times I was beaten with rods, once I was stoned, three times I was shipwrecked, a night and a day I have been in the deep; in journeys often, in perils of waters . . . in hunger and thirst . . . in cold and nakedness—besides the other things, what comes upon me daily: my anxiety for all the churches.*
> [2 Corinthians 11:24–28, New King James Bible.]

I seriously ask you, would you trade a record like that for sports cars, a constant tan, and other material pleasures that money can buy for a few temporary decades on this earth?

Joseph Smith also proved his sincerity by sacrifice. Writing to the Church during a legal persecution that kept him in hiding in and out of Nauvoo for months, he also looked back: "The envy and wrath of man have been my common lot all the days of my life . . . and I feel, like Paul, to glory in tribulation" (D&C 127:2). Why did either Paul or Joseph Smith do this? Because they positively knew the truth of the gospel, the resurrection, and the judgment, and that the riches of eternity made everything else secondary. The modern Prophet explained that his lifelong persecutions for telling his visions made him feel "much like Paul . . . [H]e was ridiculed and reviled. But all this did not destroy the reality of his vision. He had seen a vision, he knew he had, and all the persecution under heaven could not make it otherwise" (JS-H 1:24).

Many men and women sacrifice for their families and their principles. How many claim the visions of heaven and sacrifice as a witness of that? Most recent founders of successful religions live comfortably by the donations of their followers. But God's plan for his prophets tries them in fire, not only for their own postgraduate education, but for the clear validity of their testimony. Relatively few religious leaders have dared to claim visions on the level of Paul and Joseph Smith. And in the test of integrity, the quality of Joseph Smith's sacrifice clearly reaches the level of the ancient apostle. Joseph Smith's biographers will never run out of exciting copy because his life writes itself in the drama of giving for the gospel. This American prophet was too busy sacrificing to summarize all his trials, but any historian can easily take Paul's format and adapt it to Joseph Smith, who might have written:

> *A number of times Christians leveled guns at me with the threat of death. Once I was beaten, tarred, and feathered, and left unconscious. Twice I was endangered by stagecoach runaways when on the Lord's business. I have taken back roads and waded through swamps to escape my enemies. I have endured years of inconvenient travel on land for the kingdom, as well as risked many steamboat journeys on waterways. I faced years of unjust legal harassment, making my own home unsafe, and was imprisoned for a long winter in a filthy jail on unverified charges. Through all I maintained the responsibility of leading the Church, worrying, praying, and planning for the welfare of my family and my fellow Saints.*[13]

THEIR LOVE FOR THE SAINTS

Neither Paul nor Joseph Smith were strange aberrations, but vital personalities who loved and were loved. Indeed the genuineness of their selfless love is an important facet of their sacrifice for the gospel. I know of no two prophets who taught the meaning of love better than Paul and Joseph Smith. They must have been close to the Savior, who made love the foundation principle of the gospel. Indeed, the various fields of social studies recognize genuine love as the core of a healthy personality.

It is hardly necessary to comment on Paul's sketch of celestial love in 1 Corinthians 13, or his fatherly concern for cooperating and rebellious converts alike. Joseph Smith's life exhibits the same mature concern for others. For example, he could have escaped from custody at the beginning of the winter of Liberty Jail, but he would not for fear of reprisals on the Latter-day Saints. After their safety was assured by the dissipation of mobs and beginning migration, he tried three jailbreaks, all of them creative, but only the last successful. And at the end Joseph returned from the far bank of the Mississippi, observing that if his life was of no value to his people, it was of no value to himself. The historical documents surrounding this decision prove that he consciously placed himself in the danger of assassination in jail to keep angry troops from coming to Nauvoo to look for him and endanger his people. Time and again Joseph placed his safety second and the welfare of his family and Latter-day Saints first.

So there is substance in his Nauvoo teachings on love. His comments before the Relief Society are often homely in expression but godly in content: "The nearer we get to our Heavenly Father, the more we are disposed to look with compassion on perishing souls, to take them upon our shoulders, and cast their sins behind our back."[14] Earlier he had written to the Twelve on leaving home to preach the gospel: "A man filled with the love of God is not content with blessing his family alone, but ranges through the whole world, anxious to bless the whole human race."[15] I have pondered on the relationship of love and truth, an issue not very far from Keats's association of truth and beauty. The link for me is selflessness. One with true concern for you is not trying to exploit you for his benefit—thus he is most likely to give you truth and not his devious form of exploitation.

Joseph Smith gave one of his most telling insights into self just weeks before his martyrdom. Biographer Brodie thought that Joseph's "no man knows my history" hinted at deception, a 180-degree error. But this 1844 statement is really Joseph Smith's valedictory of love, linking his visions with his unlimited giving of self: "I have no enmity against any man . . . for I love all men, especially these my brethren and sisters. . . . You never knew my heart. No man knows my history. I cannot do it. I shall never undertake [it]. If I had not experienced what I have, I should not have known it myself. I never did harm any man since I have been born in the world. My voice is always for peace."[16] Joseph simply says that he knew marvelous things; therefore he shared. Can you believe a generous teacher or loving parent who

says this? Such language pierces my soul. Knowing that Joseph Smith
and Paul sincerely loved, I cannot believe that either deceived.

THEIR MARTYRDOM

There is little time for the many prophecies of Joseph Smith
and Paul. They both pass the test of pre-inspiration, a topic for
another talk and much more. There is room for a brief comment
on the prophecies of each concerning martyrdom. Both Paul and
Joseph Smith had predicted safety in earlier persecutions, but they
accurately predicted their own deaths. This is a simple translation
of that thought in Paul's final letter, 2 Timothy: "For I am already
on the point of being sacrificed; the time of my departure has come"
(2 Timothy 4:6, literal translation). From 1842 Joseph Smith had
said that his work was virtually through and he could die at any
time; in 1844 he negotiated on final arrest, bluntly telling Governor
Ford in several letters that the legal process was a pretext "till some
bloodthirsty villain could find his opportunity to shoot us."[17] Joseph
gave himself into the hands of his enemies with full knowledge
of his impending death. I am convinced on the basis of Nauvoo
sources. Contemporary journals record his forebodings on the way
to Carthage, and Willard Richards wrote the Prophet's words there
the day before martyrdom: "I have had a good deal of anxiety about
my safety, which I never did before—I could not help [it]."[18] And his
non-Mormon lawyer recalled that Joseph said on the morning of the
martyrdom "that he should not live to see another day, so fully was
he impressed with the belief that he would be murdered, all of which
proved true."[19]

What are the most important things in the world today? Do
not look for them in the media, for the three best historians of the
first century barely mention Christianity as a disreputable supersti-
tion, and no one mentions Paul. The preservation of his history and
personal letters we owe to the believers, who considered all he did
and said far more important than the Jewish wars of the century
or the aberrations of the emperors. Today's newspapers are filled
with human drama, athletic scores, political power plays, shocking

accidents, and actions of strange and often evil people. But the real news of the day they seldom carry—the outreach of the silent minority for righteousness, the moral choices of the faithful. Revelations to Paul and Joseph Smith make clear that this is the question on judgment day after all else has passed away. The devout Gandhi was shocked when told by his Christian friends "that all good works were useless." Thus he rejected such Christianity as irreligious, saying: "I do not seek redemption from the consequences of my sin. I seek to be redeemed from sin itself, or rather from the very thought of sin."[20] Through Joseph Smith the gospel was restored as originally taught by Paul, with its sweet assurance of forgiveness on condition that each believer obey the Ten Commandments and through Christ rise to perfection beyond that. Both Paul and Joseph Smith agree that perfection will come not in meditative isolation but in dynamic service, in priesthood-led programs, including the family.

THEIR COMMITMENT—AND OURS

As you read Joseph Smith's teachings and Paul's letters note the total commitment of each. Both were men consumed with a mission, which continues the question of what is really important in your world and your life. Of his work Paul said, "Necessity is laid upon me, for woe to me if I do not preach the gospel" (1 Corinthians 9:16, literal translation). One who had stood in the presence of Christ knew the urgency of each day and the real work for eternity going on around him. With the same conviction of urgency, Joseph Smith commented: "If I had not actually got into this work, and been called of God, I would back out. But I cannot back out—I have no doubt of the truth."[21] Does the spirit of revelation in you respond to the spirit of revelation in them? Do you expect to dwell with Christ, Paul, and Joseph Smith without paying the price that they paid—energetic service, discomfort, and ridicule for the cause of the Lord? The lives of these men who gave their all testify eloquently to the truth of their message. But their examples pose an inescapable question for everyone who knows what you know about them. How much will you give for the cause of the Lord? The answer can only be yours, and I pray

that you will find an inspired one—which I ask in the name of Jesus
Christ. Amen.

FOOTNOTES

1. Princeton Religion Research Center, *Emerging Trends*, April
1983.

2. Joseph Smith to Silas Smith, 26 September 1833, Kirtland,
Ohio, cit. Lucy Smith, *Biographical Sketches* (Liverpool, 1853), p. 208.

3. Parley P. Pratt, *Autobiography of Parley Pratt* (Salt Lake City:
Deseret Book Co., 1979), p. 298.

4. See Acts 22:17–21; 1 Corinthians 12:1–4, inference; Acts
18:9–10; Acts 23:11.

5. For the most accessible visions, see D&C 76:22–24; D&C
137:2–3; D&C 110:1–10.

6. Andrew F. Ehat and Lyndon W. Cook, *The Words of Joseph
Smith* (Provo, Utah: Religious Studies Center, Brigham Young
University, 1980), p. 14. Quotations from this work reproducing
journal entries may be quoted with addition of punctuation.

7. Ibid., p. 12.

8. For examples, see ibid., pp. 10, 164, 230. Other Joseph Smith
sources furnish parallels.

9. Ehat and Cook, p. 5; also *Teachings*, p. 151.

10. Joseph Smith to Emma Smith, June 6, 1832, Greenville,
Indiana, orig. at the Chicago Historical Society.

11. Ehat and Cook, p. 113.

12. For examples, see Ehat and Cook, pp. 4, 37, 62, 72, 367.
Other Joseph Smith sources furnish parallels. Cf. Hebrews 6:1–3.

13. As indicated in the text, this first-person statement is my
creation, based on what Joseph Smith could have said accurately
about his trials for the gospel.

14. Ehat and Cook, p. 123.

15. Joseph Smith to the Twelve, October 1840, Nauvoo, Ill.,
cit. *HC* 4:237.

16. Ehat and Cook, p. 355.

17. Joseph Smith to Thomas Ford, 22 June 1844, cit. *HC* 6:540.

18. Willard Richards, Joseph Smith Journal, 26 June 1844, LDS Historical Department ms.

19. Col. J. W. Woods, "The Mormon Prophet," *Daily Democrat*, Ottumwa, Iowa, 10 May 1885.

20. Mohandas K. Gandhi, *An Autobiography* (Boston: Beacon Press, 1940, 1957), p. 124.

21. Ehat and Cook, p. 179.

The Looseness of Zion:
Joseph Smith and the Lighter View

Leonard J. Arrington

This morning I should like to say a few words about things we have found in the documents in the Church Archives that bear on the life and character of Joseph Smith. During the past two years I have had the opportunity of going through the diaries, letters, and histories of the Prophet and of those associated with him. This has given me an added appreciation of Joseph Smith as a person and leader.

With respect to his life as a boy, the evidence accumulated by Richard Anderson, Marvin Hill, Dean Jessee, Ivan Barrett, and others shows that the family in which he grew up were hard workers, intelligent people, but not highly educated. They apparently prayed as a family every morning and evening, enjoyed singing hymns, read the Bible together, and were very interested in religion. The boys enjoyed homemade sports such as playing ball, wrestling, and pulling sticks. One neighbor described Joseph as "a real clever, jovial boy"; another neighbor said that the Smiths were "the best family in the neighborhood in case of sickness," and said that Young Joe, as he

Leonard J. Arrington was Church Historian for The Church of Jesus Christ of Latter-day Saints when this devotional address was given at Brigham Young University on 19 November 1974. © *Intellectual Reserve, Inc.*

called him, worked for him "and he was a good worker" (William H. and E. L. Kelley interviews, *Saints' Herald* [1881], 161–68, quoted in Richard L. Anderson, "A Corrected View of Joseph Smith's New York Reputation").

Joseph's father, it appears, reacted against the strict discipline required by the contemporary religions of the day. The devout people of his day were not many generations removed from the Puritans, and the goal set up by the ministers of the time was that each church member should become a spiritual athlete—that is, work unceasingly at being a religious person. Brigham Young, who was five years older than the Prophet, described how he was brought up:

> *When I was young* [he said], *I was kept within very strict bounds, and was not allowed to walk more than half-an-hour on Sunday for exercise.* [In fact, he said*], the proper and necessary gambols of youth* [were] *denied me. . . . I had not a chance to dance when I was young, and never heard the enchanting tones of the violin, until I was eleven years of age; and then I thought I was on the high way to hell, if I suffered myself to linger and listen to it. . . . The Christian world of my youth considered it very wicked to listen to music and to dance.* [*Journal of Discourses,* 2:94]

He went on to say that the parents of his day whipped their children for reading novels, never let them go to the theater, and prohibited them from playing or associating with other children. In his words, "They bind them to the moral law." The consequence was that duty became "loathsome," he said; "when they are freed by age from the rigorous training of their parents, they are more fit for companions to devils, than to be the children of such religious parents" (*Journal of Discourses,* 2:94).

The result of this strictness, he said, was that when such a child was in his late teens he tended to "steal away from father and mother; and when he has broken his bands," he said, "you would think all hell was let loose, and that he would compass the world at once" (*Journal of Discourses,* 2:94). He left the church and ended up not belonging to any church. (I think Milton Backman has discovered that something

like 90 percent of Joseph Smith's and Brigham Young's parents'
generation did not belong to any church [Milton V. Backman, Jr.,
American Religions and the Rise of Mormonism (Salt Lake City, 1965),
p. 283].) As for those who did belong to churches, they were so con-
ditioned by their early repressive experience that they felt guilty if
they enjoyed the ordinary things of life and expressed that guilt in a
sanctimonious demeanor and grave countenance.

"MAN IS THAT HE MIGHT HAVE JOY"

It was in such an environment that Joseph Smith grew up. But
before he went through the stage of rebellion, before the development of a guilt complex, the Lord granted to him, at the age of four-
teen, that glorious First Vision. The Lord got to him, in other words,
before the religions of the day were able to deaden his youthful exu-
berance and openness, his capacity for enjoying the mental, cultural,
and physical aspects of life. He thus avoided the artificially severe,
ascetic, fun-abhorring mantle that contemporary religion seemed to
insist upon. He was pious, but not inhibited; earnest, but not fanati-
cal; a warm, affectionate, and enjoyable personality—a prophet who
was both serious and playful—a wonderful exemplar of the precept
"Man is that he might have joy."

Jedediah M. Grant, who knew the Prophet well, underscored
this point when he declared that Joseph Smith preached against the
"super-abundant stock of sanctimoniousness" that characterized
contemporary religion. According to Elder Grant, a certain minister,
out of curiosity, came to see the Prophet in Nauvoo and carried this
sanctimonious spirit so far that the Prophet finally suggested to the
minister that they engage in a little wrestling. The minister was so
shocked that he just stood there rigid and dumbfounded, whereupon
the Prophet playfully acted as though to put him on the floor and
help him get up and then called attention to the so-called Christian
"follies" of the time, the absurdity of the long, solemn, "asslike" tone
of speaking and acting, and the dangers of excessive piety and fanati-
cism (*Journal of Discourses*, 3:66–67).

In other words, the Prophet recognized as unhealthy the mind which lacked balance, perspective, and humor. In the society of his day there were many earnest people who habitually looked on the serious side of things that had no serious side, who regarded humor as incompatible with religion. It was common for these descendants of the Puritans to see displays of humor as a mark of insincerity, for humor suggested that nothing really mattered and that life was basically comic. To be overly humorous, they thought, was to be cynical toward life. But Joseph Smith saw humor and religion as quite reconcilable. As he saw it, once one acknowledges that there is something beyond laughter—a core of life that is solemn, serious, and tender—there is still plenty of room for jesting. At least, that is the way he was—"a jolly good fellow," as one contemporary described him.

That this is the way Joseph Smith turned out there can be no doubt. We have a number of contemporary descriptions of him. One person, after meeting him, said, "He possesses the innate refinement that one finds in the born poet or in the most highly cultivated intellectual." Another found him a "sociable, easy, cheerful, obliging, kind, and hospitable person." Another described him as "kind and considerate, taking a personal interest in all people, considering everyone his equal." Still another describes him as "a fine, noble looking man." All of this suggests that he had a balanced, well-adjusted, healthy personality and that people enjoyed being around him and he them.

THE PROPHET'S JOVIAL NATURE

Joseph was confident and sure of himself but did not take himself more seriously than the circumstances warranted. As recorded in the Sermons of Joseph Smith file at the Church Archives, he said in 1843, "I am not a very pious man [in terms of the superpiety of Christian ministers of his day]. I do not wish to be a great deal better than anybody else" (compare *History of the Church*, 5:401). Then he went on to explain that he enjoyed being with people, wanted to be with them as well in the hereafter, and thus did not wrap himself in a pious rectitude which would separate him from his brothers and sisters.

Emma's lot must have been a difficult one, for he was always bringing home a group to dinner. But she was a good cook. "When I want a little bread and milk," Joseph told William W. Phelps, "my wife loads the table with so many good things it destroys my appetite." The Prophet enjoyed his family. There are dozens of references in his official diary that read like this one of March 27, 1834: "Remained at home and had great joy with my family." Indeed, according to a cousin, George A. Smith, one convert family apostatized because, when they arrived in Kirtland from the East, Joseph came downstairs from the room "where he had been translating by the gift and power of God" and began to romp and play with his children (*Journal of Discourses*, 2:214). In their view, this was not proper behavior for a prophet! The Prophet's journal mentions going with his family to musical concerts, the theater, and circus performances, and taking excursions on Mississippi riverboats.

Joseph's well-adjusted nature was infectious. Those brought up in the strict, long-faced, pious tradition soon found themselves liberated so they could fulfill their foreordained roles of being leaders of the Saints. Converts who had been brought up with less enjoyment of life and spontaneity were unfrozen; their experiences and enjoyments were expanded. The wholesome healthiness of Joseph Smith, in other words, brought changes in the unhealthy piety and smugness and sanctimoniousness of others who were benefited by association with him. Religion was not to *confine* spirits, he pointed out, but to *expand* them. Direct experience with the Prophet gave them reassurance of the fuller and more joyful life the gospel called for them to live.

Brigham Young, for example, despite his pious upbringing, learned to dance, very stately to be sure, learned to be an actor (he played the part of the High Priest in "Pizarro"), and in short enjoyed life and helped those associated with him to enjoy life, despite their many trials and problems. No wonder Brigham Young said, "I feel like shouting hallelujah, all the time, when I think that I ever knew Joseph Smith, the Prophet" (*Journal of Discourses*, 3:51).

Because of this spontaneity, joviality, and combination of seriousness of purpose and good humor, everybody was quickly attracted
to Joseph Smith. His religion, revelations, and spirituality attracted
them, of course, but so did his person, and converts did not fail to
mention this in their diaries and letters. In fact, meeting him for the
first time was such a momentous occasion that nearly everyone who
kept a diary or wrote his life history recorded that first encounter, as
if it were the greatest event of their lives—which, of course, for many
of them it was!

WORK AND RECREATION IN THE EARLY CHURCH

When Brigham Young and his brother Joseph Young went to
see Joseph Smith in 1832, "they found him chopping wood, for [as
Wilford Woodruff said] he was a labouring man, and gained his bread
by the sweat of his brow." The Prophet, according to the account
of this meeting, "received them gladly, invited them to his house,
and they rejoiced together in the Gospel of Christ, and their hearts
were knitted together in the spirit and bond of union" (*Journal of
Discourses*, 7:100).

When Wilford Woodruff first met the Prophet in April 1834 at
Kirtland, he wrote:

*I saw him out in the field with his brother Hyrum: he had on a very old
hat. . . . I was introduced to him, and he invited me home with him.*

*I accepted the invitation, and I watched him pretty closely, to see what
I could learn. He remarked, while passing to his house, that this was the first
hour he had spent in recreation for a long time.*

*Shortly after we arrived at his house, he went into an adjoining room,
and brought out a wolf-skin, and said, "Brother Woodruff, I want you to
help me to tan this." So I pulled off my coat, went to work and helped him,
and felt honoured in so doing. He was about going up with the brethren to
redeem Zion, and he wanted this wolf-skin to put upon his waggon seat, as
he had no buffalo robe. . . . Well, we tanned it, and used it. . . . This was
my first introduction to the Prophet Joseph Smith. . . . I rejoiced to behold*

his face and to hear his voice. I was fully satisfied that Joseph was a Prophet. [*Journal of Discourses*, 7:101; also *Millennial Star* 53 (1891): 627–28]).

Brother Woodruff had reason later on to expand that first impression. After long association with the Prophet, he wrote: "I have felt to rejoice exceedingly in what I saw of brother Joseph, for in his public and private career he carried with him the Spirit of the Almighty, and he manifested a greatness of soul which I had never seen in any other man" (*Journal of Discourses*, 7:101).

Joseph Smith had a humanizing influence on others, like Parley and Orson Pratt and Orson Hyde. Orson Hyde, for example, began one of his sermons by admitting that he had sometimes spoken too loudly and energetically and promised:

I shall endeavor, the Lord being my helper, to modulate my voice according to the Spirit of God that I may have when speaking, and not go beyond it, neither fall short. At the same time, I do not want my mind so trammeled as brother Parley P. Pratt's once was, when dancing was first introduced into Nauvoo among the Saints. I observed brother Parley standing in the figure, and he was making no motion particularly, only up and down. Says I, "Brother Parley, why don't you move forward?" Says he, "When I think which way I am going, I forget the step; and when I think of the step, I forget which way to go." [Journal of Discourses, 6:150]

The apostasy of people who saw the Prophet interspersing times of spiritual communion with periods of boisterous activity is an illustration of the teachings of his time about levity supposedly being in conflict with piety. In contrast, thousands of converts found the experience of living with the Saints in Kirtland and Nauvoo and in the Salt Lake Valley to be exhilarating. Mormonism loosened them up, as it were. From the tense and humorless pursuit of immediate goals, it gave them balance and caused them to enjoy earthly life, even when filled with sorrow and frustration. The atmosphere around Joseph was one of hope and buoyancy, of optimism and faith, of wholesome righteousness, and yet there was a loosening of the strict bonds of contemporary Calvinism.

Joseph Smith helped teach people what true religion was, and he taught them very graphically that it was *not* sanctimoniousness (*Journal of Discourses*, 3:66–67). Not only that, he taught them that it was something which expanded their lives and potentials in the way his was expanded.

Listen to the kind of recreation the Saints held under the Prophet's direction in Nauvoo: On February 20, 1843, a "wood-cutting bee" was held at the Prophet's home. Seventy brethren attended. They sawed, chopped, split, and piled up a large stack of wood in the yard, which served not only the Prophet's family, but also the many persons they helped out. "The day was spent by them with much pleasantry, good humor and feeling," says the record. "A white oak log, measuring five feet four inches in diameter was cut through with a cross-cut saw, in four-and-a-half minutes, by Hyrum Dayton and brother John Tidwell." This tree had been previously cut by the Prophet himself, and he had hauled it to the yard with his team (Joseph Smith, *History of the Church*, 5:282).

Joseph said that once when he was in his office, he saw two boys fighting in the street. He ran out, "caught one of the boys (who had begun the fight with clubs,) and then the other; and, after giving them proper instruction," as he termed it, "gave the bystanders a lecture" for egging the boys on instead of stopping the fight, and finally concluded the matter by saying that nobody was allowed to fight in Nauvoo but himself (*History of the Church*, 5:282-83). Joseph Smith favored music, drama, debating, hiking, boating, athletics, parties, dancing, and picnics. He liked going for long walks, horseback riding, and getting out into the beauty of nature. Here is the account of his activities for Wednesday, February 8, 1843:

This morning, I read German, and visited with a brother and sister from Michigan, who thought that "a prophet is always a prophet;" but I told them that a prophet was a prophet only when he was acting as such. After dinner Brother Parley P. Pratt came in: we had conversation on various subjects. At four in the afternoon, I went out with my little [son] *Frederick, to exercise myself by sliding on the ice.* [*History of the Church*, 5:265]

THE BALANCE OF SERIOUSNESS AND HUMOR

One could misunderstand all this. It is easy to carry the epicurean philosophy too far. One needs the help of the Spirit in drawing the line between living the fuller life to which we are called by the gospel and indulging in licentious behavior. The Prophet himself prayed for guidance on this principle. As with all of us, this greatest of all prophets prayed for forgiveness of his excesses, for his personal salvation. To use his own expression in a letter to Emma, "I pray that I may steer my own bark safe" (Joseph Smith to Emma Smith, 21 March 1839, Church Archives). The point I am making is that the Prophet was also concerned about extremes—becoming so concerned about the danger of overexuberance that one swings the pendulum back and focuses too heavily on repressing wrong desires. For Joseph did insist on self-control and righteous living. He was not the happy-go-lucky companion who would let his friends get away with anything: "The Saints need not think because I am familiar with them and am playful and cheerful, that I am ignorant of what is going on," he said on one occasion. "Iniquity of any kind cannot be sustained in the Church, and it will not fare well where I am; for I am determined while I do lead the Church, to lead it right" (quoted in Wilford Woodruff journal, *History of the Church*, 5:411).

Certainly the calling of prophet was one of such high seriousness that its responsibilities could well have weighted down a less vital mind. But it was humor which helped Joseph to dispose of conflicts and problems that did not really matter. The Prophet was deeply serious, but he was not solemn; he believed an unduly solemn person had lost something of the image of his Creator.

What he was teaching the Saints in all of this, it seems to me, is something equivalent to what psychologists have referred to as the principle or law of reversed effect. This says that often our efforts to keep from doing a wrong thing are so tense and determined that they magnify our chances of doing that very thing. Paul discovered this principle when he wrote to the Romans, "I find then a law, that, when I would do good, evil is present with me" (Romans 7:21). Our difficult moral struggles require a certain relaxation and surrender. We should give the Lord and the Holy Ghost a chance to do the refreshing. This principle of relaxed enjoyment and acceptance of life, rather than tense struggle to achieve perfection, fits in with the design of the Lord's purpose, "Man is that he might have joy." This, it seems to me, is one of the things the Prophet was trying to get across. And this principle is particularly important to those of us who are a little older—as, for example, graduate students, for it is at this time that we are likely to discover the gap between our earlier aspirations and our abilities. We all have exaggerated expectations of life, and sooner or later we discover that we are less clever than we had thought, that we have to be satisfied with less income, less popularity, even a less ideal marriage than we had hoped for. In an unhealthy situation this leads to resentment, projection of blame, distress, and maladjustment. The Latter-day Saint has an ideal background for coping with this situation as he adjusts his ambitions to the place in life which the Lord has in store for him.

I pray that as individuals and as families we may laugh together, just as we pray together; that we may recognize our heritage, its few weaknesses along with its great strengths, without fear; that we may develop the cultural pride which others will expect of the Lord's chosen people; that we may appreciate the wonderfully warm and engaging persons that all of our prophets have been; and that we may continue to exhibit that loyalty to the principles of the gospel that would make the angels in heaven rejoice. And I pray this in the name of Jesus, the Christ. Amen.

What Came from Kirtland

M. Russell Ballard

Sister Ballard and I appreciate, more than words can express, being here with all of you tonight. Please know of our love and concern for each one of you. It's a wonderful thing to reach across the footprint of the satellite and gather close to the young adults of the Church. I pray that the Lord will bless me that I may have his spirit with me tonight. I have worked hard on the preparation for what I'd like to say to you. If we have the spirit of the Lord with us, perhaps we will all learn something that is worthwhile.

During this past year I was privileged to have two special experiences that have affected me deeply. One was a leadership meeting in historic Kirtland, Ohio, with Church leaders from 109 stakes and districts and 24 missions in the northeastern United States and Canada. The other was being in Nauvoo and Carthage, Illinois, with President Howard W. Hunter and President Gordon B. Hinckley to commemorate the 150th anniversary of the martyrdom of the Prophet Joseph and his brother Hyrum. I cannot adequately express the depth of my feelings of love and gratitude to these great men.

M. Russell Ballard was a member of the Quorum of the Twelve Apostles of The Church of Jesus Christ of Latter-day Saints when this fireside address was given at Brigham Young University on 6 November 1994. © Intellectual Reserve, Inc.

As we visited Carthage Jail, where Joseph and Hyrum were murdered, and the beautiful Smith Family Cemetery overlooking the wide Mississippi River where they are buried, I stood in reverential awe. I pay tribute to these noble brothers, my great-great-uncle Joseph and my great-great-grandfather Hyrum. I pay tribute to them for their faith and courage to sacrifice all they had, even their lives, by sealing their missions and their testimonies with their blood.

It is a blessing to know that Joseph and Hyrum, who "in life . . . were not divided, and in death . . . were not separated" (D&C 135:3), were instruments through whom the Lord restored his church in our day.

Tonight I would like to concentrate on the remarkable events of the Restoration that occurred in and near Kirtland, Ohio, where Joseph and Hyrum lived for seven years and where Joseph spent the majority of his adult life. It is often said that the Kirtland period is one of the least-understood periods in Church history. Kirtland is truly a holy ground of this dispensation. The Church basks in the light of revelation today to a great extent because of the great Pentecostal outpouring that Joseph and the Saints received in Kirtland.

The heavens literally opened to hundreds of our early Saints there. For many weeks surrounding the Kirtland Temple dedication, the Savior, past prophets, and angels communed directly with Joseph and Hyrum and other great leaders of our dispensation. Joseph prophesied that these Pentecostal events would "be handed down . . . to all generations" and that we should celebrate them as a "year of jubilee, and time of rejoicing" (*HC* 2:432–33).

It has been said that we may yet discover that Kirtland is our most significant Church history site. Let me describe to you how important Kirtland is to the Church. In Kirtland were revealed basically all of the priesthood offices that we have in the Church today. This was the schooling period for the leaders of the Church. About one-half of the revelations recorded in the Doctrine and Covenants were revealed there, far more than at any other location. There in Kirtland is where the School of the Prophets began. There is where

Joseph made his Bible translation. There is where the Pearl of Great Price was largely translated. There is where the first edition of the Doctrine and Covenants was printed.

More heavenly manifestations occurred in Kirtland than in any other place. For example, in Kirtland the Father and the Son appeared or were seen in vision four times, and the Savior was seen at least six more times by Joseph Smith. In Kirtland is where significant keys were given. The Church headquartered in Kirtland longer than in anywhere else except Salt Lake City. We built our first temple and completed our first temple ordinances in Kirtland. Time allows me to review only four sacred spots that we visited one year ago this month.

We first visited the Whitney store, where about twenty sections of our Doctrine and Covenants, including our Word of Wisdom, were received. This store served jointly as Joseph and Emma's home as well as the Church Office Building from 1832–1834. It was our first bishops' storehouse. I wish you could feel the same spirit we felt in that small School of the Prophets room in the Whitney store. It is just 11 feet x 14 feet in size. The heavens opened to about twenty men in that room as the words of the Lord authorized the organization of the First Presidency in our day. Many saw the Savior. Both the Father and Son were present as well as concourses of angels that day. I stood in the translating room (which is next to the School of the Prophets room) with three other stake and mission presidents whose forefathers were also in that same room with mine in 1832. We contemplated how our ancestors Joseph Smith, Sr., Hyrum Smith, Orson Hyde, Frederick G. Williams, and Newel K. Whitney felt as they watched Joseph dictate section 88 of the Doctrine and Covenants.

The second place we visited was the Johnson farm in Hiram, Ohio, just a few miles from Kirtland. In the revelation room of the Johnson home, the heavens opened and sixteen revelations came to the Prophet Joseph Smith. It was in that small room that God the Father and Jesus Christ appeared to Joseph and Sidney Rigdon. They testified of Christ as they exclaimed,

This is the testimony, last of all, which we give of him: That he lives!
For we saw him, even on the right hand of God. [D&C 76:22–23]

We contemplated what it must have been like to have been one of
the dozen men who were present in that room on that occasion and
saw Joseph "in the midst of a magnificent glory." Although they were
not permitted to see the vision, they testified they "saw the glory and
felt the power" (Philo Dibble, "Recollections of the Prophet Joseph
Smith," *Juvenile Instructor* 27, 15 May 1892, pp. 303–4).

Our hearts were touched as we stood in Joseph and Emma's small
bedroom in the Johnson home and visualized twelve out of a mob of
over fifty who burst into that bedroom and dragged Joseph from his
bed on that cold night and carried him to the meadow, where they
tarred and feathered him and without mercy beat him. All night the
tar and feathers were removed. Joseph suffered great pain, and yet
he preached to the crowd the next day and, after preaching, baptized
three individuals. We stood in reverence on that same porch and
pondered the power and strength of the Prophet Joseph.

At the third place we walked up the hill behind the Morley farm
and stood in a grove of trees, contemplating the vision of the Father
and the Son received by Joseph and two other brethren in the little
log schoolhouse that used to stand there. Here Joseph ordained the
first high priests in our dispensation. The adversary tried to prevent
the ordinations that day. As Joseph cast the evil influence out, a great
vision opened to him, and he exclaimed, "I now see God, and Jesus
Christ at his right hand, let them kill me, I should not feel death
as I am now" ("The Life of Levi Hancock," copied from his own
journal by Clara E. H. Lloyd, typescript, Historical Department, The
Church of Jesus Christ of Latter-day Saints, p. 33).

Wilford Woodruff recorded an experience in that little log
schoolhouse as follows:

On Sunday night the Prophet called on all who held the Priesthood to
gather into the little log school house they had there. It was a small house,
perhaps 14 feet square. But it held the whole of the Priesthood of the Church

*of Jesus Christ of Latter-day Saints who were then in the town of Kirtland,
and who had gathered together to go off in Zion's camp. . . . The Prophet
called upon the Elders of Israel with him to bear testimony of this work. . . .
And a good many . . . bore their testimonies. When they got through the
Prophet said, "Brethren I have been very much edified and instructed in
your testimonies here tonight, but I want to say to you before the Lord, that
you know no more concerning the destinies of this Church and kingdom than
a babe upon its mother's lap. You don't comprehend it." I was rather sur-
prised. He said, "It is only a little handful of Priesthood you see here tonight,
but this Church will fill North and South America—it will fill the world."*
[*CR*, April 1898, p. 57]

Perhaps Joseph saw congregations of priesthood and faithful
sisters assembled as we are tonight. It was in Kirtland that he proph-
esied that we would build temples in the Rocky Mountains (Wilford
Woodruff, *CR*, April 1898, p. 57). Hyrum Smith also prophesied in
Kirtland that the Saints would go to the Rocky Mountains (Lorenzo
Dow Young, "Lorenzo Dow Young's Narrative," in *Fragments of
Experience: Sixth Book of the Faith Promoting Series* [Salt Lake City:
Juvenile Instructor Office, 1882], p. 44).

On that beautiful Morley farm we read inspirational verses from
thirteen sections of our Doctrine and Covenants that were given
there. We considered what it would have been like to have been
present as Joseph dictated those marvelous revelations from the Lord.
Can you imagine the feeling the Saints experienced as Joseph dictated
these words of the Savior: "I am Jesus that was crucified. I am the
Son of God" (D&C 45:52) or "I am in your midst, and I am the good
shepherd" (D&C 50:44) or

*Behold, I will go before you and be your rearward; and I will be in your
midst, and you shall not be confounded.*
Behold, I am Jesus Christ, and I come quickly. [D&C 49:27–28]

Witnessing this rich outpouring of heavenly instruction in
Kirtland bore an unwavering witness to most of those early Saints
of this: that the Lord Jesus Christ led this Church!

Finally, the fourth place was where we had the humbling and
overwhelming experience of sitting in the Kirtland Temple, the site
of some of the greatest spiritual events of this, the dispensation of the
fulness of times. Can you imagine what it would have been like for
the Prophet Joseph and Oliver Cowdery to see "the blazing throne of
God, whereon was seated the Father and the Son" (D&C 137:3) or
to see "the Lord standing upon the breastwork of the pulpit" (D&C
110:2) and to hear him say, "Your sins are forgiven you; you are clean
before me; therefore, lift up your heads and rejoice" (D&C 110:5) or
to witness the visit of seven prophets of past dispensations? Can you
imagine their feelings on dedication day as they saw the apostle Peter
come into the upper pulpits and sit between Joseph Smith, Sr., and
Frederick G. Williams? The reality of this experience is captured by
Heber C. Kimball as he described Peter in detail. He said Peter was
"very tall . . . , [had] black eyes, white hair, and stoop[ed] shoulder[s];
his garment was whole, extending to near his ankles; on his feet he
had sandals" (Orson F. Whitney, *Life of Heber C. Kimball* [Salt Lake
City: Bookcraft, 1967], p. 91). Brother Kimball also recounted how
John the Beloved appeared to several in the Kirtland Temple near the
same time.

Can you imagine how the Prophet Joseph and Oliver Cowdery
must have felt as Moses, Elias, and Elijah appeared to them and
committed keys, dispensations, and sealing powers there—not unlike
what occurred on the Mount of Transfiguration about two thousand
years before.

In addition to these experiences, we reviewed some of the
sixty-five revelations given in Ohio. I was reminded how boldly the
Lord spoke. In section 1 of the Doctrine and Covenants, the Lord
straightforwardly declared,

Behold, I am God and have spoken it; these commandments are of
me. . . .

Search these commandments, for they are true . . . and the prophecies
and promises which are in them shall all be fulfilled.
What I the Lord have spoken, I have spoken, and I excuse not myself.
[D&C 1:24, 37–38]

Let me share with you some of the light and doctrine the Lord
showered on the Church in Kirtland. These are the words of the
Lord on just a few of our important doctrines.

1. On priesthood:

All they who receive this priesthood receive me. . . .
 And he that receiveth me receiveth my Father;
 And he that receiveth my Father receiveth my Father's kingdom;
therefore all that my Father hath shall be given unto him. [D&C 84:35,
37–38]

2. On obedience and keeping the commandments: "For I the
Lord cannot look upon sin with the least degree of allowance" (D&C
1:31) or "Entangle not yourselves in sin, but let your hands be clean"
(D&C 88:86) or

Unto him that keepeth my commandments I will give the mysteries of my
kingdom, and the same shall be in him a well of living water, springing up
unto everlasting life. [D&C 63:23]

3. On repentance: "He that repents and does the commandments
of the Lord shall be forgiven" (D&C 1:32).

4. On forgiving others: "I, the Lord, will forgive whom I will
forgive, but of you it is required to forgive all men" (D&C 64:10).

5. On prayer: "Draw near unto me and I will draw near unto you"
(D&C 88:63) or "Pray always lest that wicked one have power in you,
and remove you out of your place" (D&C 93:49) or also

If thou shalt ask, thou shalt receive revelation upon revelation,
knowledge upon knowledge, that thou mayest know the mysteries and

peaceable things—that which bringeth joy, that which bringeth life eternal. [D&C 42:61]

6. On pride versus humility: "Be thou humble; and the Lord thy God shall lead thee by the hand, and give thee answer to thy prayers" (D&C 112:10).

7. On healing the sick:

And the elders of the church, two or more, shall be called, and shall pray for and lay their hands upon [the sick] *in my name. . . .*

. . . He that hath faith in me to be healed, and is not appointed unto death, shall be healed. [D&C 42:44, 48]

8. On fulfilling our callings:

Let every man learn his duty, and to act in the office in which he is appointed, in all diligence.

He that is slothful shall not be counted worthy to stand, and he that learns not his duty and shows himself not approved shall not be counted worthy to stand. [D&C 107:99–100]

9. On God's love and closeness to us:

Ye have not as yet understood how great blessings the Father hath . . . prepared for you.

And ye cannot bear all things now; nevertheless, be of good cheer, for I will lead you along. The kingdom is yours and the blessings thereof are yours, and the riches of eternity are yours. [D&C 78:17–18]

Almost all the doctrine and the principles of the gospel appear in the revelations received in and around Kirtland.

In Kirtland the Lord gave us perhaps the clearest and most concise definition of the gospel when he said,

This is the gospel. . . .

That [Jesus] came into the world . . . to be crucified for the world, and to bear the sins of the world, and to sanctify the world, and to cleanse it from all unrighteousness;

That through him all might be saved whom the Father had put into his power and made by him. [D&C 76:40–42]

Think of the great charter of the Church Educational System that comes from Kirtland: "The glory of God is intelligence, or, in other words, light and truth" (D&C 93:36).

As we consider "light and truth," let me review with you in more depth what some have termed our most significant revelation to man—section 76 of the Doctrine and Covenants, which is often referred to as The Vision.

I believe that receiving this vision may have been one of the Prophet Joseph's most powerful and significant spiritual experiences. As Joseph and Sidney Rigdon prayed to understand the resurrection of the just and the unjust, this glorious vision—or actually a series of six visions—burst upon them. Joseph and Sidney literally conversed with the Lord for about one and a half hours as the Savior showed them what Joseph later said was "Eternity sketch'd in a vision from God, of what was, and now is, and yet is to be" (*Times and Seasons* 4 [1 February 1843], p. 82). As it commenced, Joseph and Sidney viewed the glory of the Son on the right hand of the Father. They also beheld angels surrounding them. They were moved to exclaim, "He lives! For we saw him" (D&C 76:22–23).

They next saw Lucifer in the premortal world as he fell from the presence of God because of his rebellion. They then saw the sons of perdition and what will happen to them. Next they viewed visions of the celestial, terrestrial, and telestial kingdoms. They learned the requirements for attaining each of these kingdoms. They learned that those who qualify "shall dwell in the presence of God and his Christ forever and ever" (D&C 76:62). They also perceived the differences in glory of these worlds. I wonder if in mortality we will ever fully realize the power and significance of this vision. Section 76 includes ten references to the conversations between the Savior and Joseph and Sidney. My dear young friends, can you imagine what you could learn if you spent one and a half hours in the presence of the Lord conversing with him and essentially having him conduct us on a guided tour of the premortal life, this earth life, and life after death? The knowledge Joseph received on the premortal existence has answered unnumbered gospel questions regarding the Council in Heaven and the creation of this world.

Joseph was commanded not to record everything that he saw in vision. As we look at his later teachings, we see what appear to be bits and pieces of this same great revelation being taught as the Saints were prepared to receive them. You see, the Prophet Joseph was not able to teach the Saints everything that he knew because they were not prepared. That is why education is constantly stressed by the Lord. That is why we encourage you to gain spiritual education by taking institute and religion classes. It is why we counsel you to read scriptures every day. It is why the Lord established the School of the Prophets. The Lord said we cannot be saved in ignorance. Can you see that this great vision described in section 76 was essentially a well from which Joseph drew pearls of knowledge throughout his life and taught the Saints as they were prepared to accept and to understand? Just think what we might be taught even today if we were prepared to receive it.

One of the key principles in section 76 is that in our pursuit of knowledge and understanding we can be taught individually through "the power of the Holy Spirit." The Lord said that this blessing can come to each of us as we "love him, and purify [our]selves before him" (D&C 76:116). I invite each of you to read section 76 with the spirit of wanting to understand what the Lord is teaching us.

Can you imagine what it would have been like to watch Joseph Smith receive these great revelations? He often had more than ten people in his presence. Many of these bore witness of the Spirit and the outward manifestations that were present as these revelations came to him. Typically they spoke of a whiteness or brightness that surrounded Joseph. For example, as section 76 was given, Philo

Dibble wrote that Joseph "seemed to be dressed in an element of glorious white, and his face shone as if it were transparent" ("Early Scenes in Church History," *Four Faith Promoting Classics* [Salt Lake City: Bookcraft, 1968], p. 81). Orson Pratt was present when section 51 was received, and he testified that "Joseph's face was exceedingly white, and seemed to shine" (*Millennial Star* 36 [11 August 1874], p. 498). Brigham Young testified,

Those who were acquainted with him knew when the Spirit of revelation was upon him, for his countenance wore an expression peculiar to himself while under that influence. He preached by the Spirit of revelation, and taught in his council by it, and those who were acquainted with him could discover it at once, for at such times there was a peculiar clearness and transparency in his face. [JD 9:89]

Many were impressed with how smoothly these revelations from the Lord flowed and how, except for minor corrections such as spelling or punctuation, they required no correcting. Parley P. Pratt said,

Each sentence was uttered slowly and very distinctly, and with a pause between each, sufficiently long for it to be recorded, by an ordinary writer, in long hand.

. . . There was never any hesitation, reviewing, or reading back, in order to keep the run of the subject; neither did any of these communications undergo revisions, interlinings, or corrections. As he dictated them so they stood, so far as I have witnessed; and I was present to witness the dictation of several communications of several pages each. [PPP, 1985, p. 48]

Those who knew Joseph best were the most astonished at this process. It was beyond Joseph's natural ability and schooling to be able to dictate such revelations from God.

One of Joseph's companions, an educator, testified to this in amazement:

I have known [Joseph and his scribe] *to seat themselves, & without premeditation, . . . deliver off in broken sentences, some of the most sublime pieces of composition which I ever perused in any book.* [William E. McLellin, *The Ensign of Liberty of the Church of Christ* 1, no. 7 (August 1849), pp. 98–99]

Emma, the one who knew Joseph best, marveled that during the Book of Mormon translation, which occurred barely three years before most of the Kirtland revelations, Joseph "could neither write nor dictate a coherent and well-worded letter; let alone dictating a book like the Book of Mormon" (or no doubt the Doctrine and Covenants or Pearl of Great Price). She then testified, "It is marvelous to me, 'a marvel and a wonder,' as much so as to anyone else" ("Last Testimony of Sister Emma," *Saints Herald* 26, no. 19 [1 October 1879], p. 290).

Emma's testimony is similar to Parley Pratt's as she continued to be amazed at the process by which revelations came. She said in an interview near the end of her life,

I am satisfied that no man could have dictated the writing of the manuscripts unless he was inspired; for, when acting as his scribe, [Joseph] *would dictate to me hour after hour; and when returning after meals, or after interruptions, he would at once begin where he had left off, without either seeing the manuscript or having any portion of it read to him. This was a usual thing for him to do. It would have been improbable that a learned man could do this; and, for one so ignorant and unlearned as he was, it was simply impossible.* [Ibid.]

The revelations in the Doctrine and Covenants were received through the power of God similar to the Book of Mormon translation.

My young brothers and sisters, can you sense how great a miracle it is that we have the Book of Mormon, the Doctrine and Covenants, and the Pearl of Great Price? They are not man-made books but the literal word of God to us. As the Lord said,

These words are not of men nor of man, but of me; wherefore, you shall
testify they are of me and not of man;
For it is my voice which speaketh them unto you. [D&C 18:34–35]

It was often difficult for those in the 1830s to accept that the
Lord spoke to them—as it is for many in our day, especially for those
who call themselves intellectuals. It should not have been, but it was.
One of the early "intellectuals" of the Church, William McLellin,
was humbled when he decided to test Joseph Smith. He wanted some
outward proof that these revelations came from God. He formulated
in his mind five questions that he wanted answered that only the Lord
and he would know. Without telling Joseph Smith the questions, he
requested a revelation. We can read the result of this inquiry in section 66 of the Doctrine and Covenants. The Lord gave this section
in answer to these five questions that only McLellin and the Lord
knew. It may be interesting for you to determine if you can discover
what these five questions were. As Joseph dictated that revelation,
McLellin got the confirmation he sought. He then recorded his personal testimony of the divine calling of the Prophet Joseph. He said,

I now testify in the fear of God, that every question [was] *answered to*
my full and entire satisfaction. I desired it for a testimony of Joseph's
inspiration. And I to this day consider it to me an evidence which I cannot
refute. [*Ensign of Liberty*, p. 61]

Joseph Smith is a true Prophet . . . of the Lord and . . . has power and
does receive revelations from God. [Letter from William E. McLellin to
relatives, 4 August 1832, RLDS Archives, p. 4]

In spite of this witness, McLellin left the Church.

There is a lesson to be learned from the study of the Doctrine
and Covenants. Revelations are generally answers to questions. The
Lord did not come and tap Joseph on the shoulder and say, "I have
a revelation for you." But instead Joseph went to the Lord and asked
to receive an answer. Time after time Joseph tells us how he would

ask and how, in response, the revelation would come. Elder Russell Nelson recently expanded on this important principle. He said, "The Lord can only teach an inquiring mind." What an important lesson. The Lord doesn't generally come to us—he waits for us to come to him and ask. Then he gives us the answer. How many times have you said, "I have not received direction lately" or "I feel a void in my life." Do we inquire of the Lord? Do we ask, seek, and knock as the Savior directed? As you have problems and questions in your lives, do you follow this principle? I testify to you that as your minds are opened and as you truly inquire of the Lord, he will answer you. As we humble ourselves, he will lead us by the hand and give us answers to our prayers.

These early years in our history literally served as a refiner's fire for early Church members. These were days of great testing when many failed the test. Leaders that survived these early days—such as Brigham Young, John Taylor, Wilford Woodruff, Lorenzo Snow, and Heber C. Kimball—were perhaps thereby enabled to survive the almost insurmountable trials of crossing the plains and establishing the Church in the Rocky Mountains. I hope that we never forget the heritage that we have from these early days.

I also pay tribute to the faithful who followed the early leaders. Think of men like John Tanner. Brother Tanner was probably the equivalent of a millionaire in the 1830s—perhaps the wealthiest man in the whole Church. He sacrificed everything so that the Kirtland Temple could be built and the Church established. After laying all of his worldly goods on the altar, he left Kirtland for Missouri in poverty with a cart, a borrowed wagon, one horse of his own, three borrowed ones, and twenty dollars in cash. When he had spent his few dollars, he begged for buttermilk and other food to sustain his family of eleven. One of his cherished daughters died during the exodus from Kirtland. Apostates taunted John Tanner because he remained faithful. His response echoed the feelings of these early faithful Saints. He said, "Well, if others have come up easier, they have not learned so much" (John Tanner, "Sketch of an Elder's Life," in *Scraps of Biography* [Salt Lake City: Juvenile Instructor Office, 1883], p. 15).

Consider also the example of Artemus Millet. In 1832 the Church faced a real dilemma. A stonemason was needed to direct the stonework on the Kirtland Temple. No one was qualified. Lorenzo Young suggested that they recruit Artemus Millet, who was a capable stonemason living in Canada. But there was one problem—Artemus was not a member of the Church. Joseph Smith paused and considered the suggestion. He then turned to Brigham Young and said, "I give you a mission to go to Canada and baptize Brother Artemus Millet and bring him here." If that wasn't enough, he then said, "And tell him to bring a thousand dollars with him" (Millet Family History, "A Brief History of Artemus Millet," manuscript, LDS Archives, pp. 70–71). You prospective and returned missionaries, how would you like to receive such a mission assignment? With the help of the Lord, Brigham Young went to Canada and taught and baptized Brother Millet. When he was asked to leave Canada to supervise the work on the Kirtland Temple, Brother Millet responded that he had a business in Canada and if he left, not only would the business fail, but people who owed him money would never pay their debts to him. Being touched by the Spirit, Brother Millet left his business and moved to Kirtland, Ohio.

The stately Kirtland Temple is in a large part a monument to Artemus Millet. He lost his business. He lost his money. He lost his prestigious standing in Canada. Later his wife died. But look what he gained. He gained the gospel. He fulfilled an important earthly mission. He gained an eternal family, and today there are thousands of his descendants in the Church who call him blessed. I know some of his descendants who are leaders in this Church and who acknowledge that much of what they count dear in their lives is because of their faithful forefathers in following the prophet of God.

My dear brothers and sisters, can you see the importance of the Kirtland period that we have discussed tonight? As I conclude, may I share with you a never-to-be-forgotten experience I had in presiding at a sacrament meeting in the Kirtland Temple. President Wallace

B. Smith of the RLDS Church graciously granted permission for us to hold a sacrament meeting in the temple. Not since the 1840s had the sacrament been blessed and passed to Latter-day Saints. We felt a power and a spirit there that may have been comparable to that felt in some of those meetings in the 1830s. When the General Authorities blessed and passed the sacrament, the Lord poured out his Spirit upon all those in attendance. These leaders today are also giving their all to build the Church in our day. The Lord blessed us with spiritual power and renewed testimonies of this work. While singing "The Spirit of God," that great hymn written for the dedication of the Kirtland Temple, all in attendance had feelings that will never be forgotten. Most all were wiping away the tears streaming down their cheeks. We were aware on that occasion of how close those on the other side of the veil are to us.

Now, my beloved young people, we love you. You have a great destiny in this Church. Study the scriptures. Study the revelations. Anchor your hearts to the great message of the restoration of the gospel of Jesus Christ. As you do this, I promise you, in the name of the Lord Jesus Christ and by and through the authority of the holy apostleship invested in me, that you will come to know the Lord, and the more you come to know him the easier your life will become. That may sound strange to you, but as an apostle, I walk the face of the earth, going wherever I am sent, and I know of the power of the Lord to bless his Saints. Sister Ballard and I will leave on Thursday for Brazil. It does not matter where we are. Those who have an unwavering testimony that Joseph Smith is a prophet of the living God know that he, in fact, received revelation from God. They know that those revelations contain all the instruction necessary for us to find peace and happiness in this life. Understand the gospel and keep the commandments of the Lord Jesus Christ and you will prosper.

I testify to you that Jesus Christ lives. He is the Son of God. This is his Church. He has spoken to his prophets. He speaks today. He is guiding the affairs of the kingdom. God bless you to keep your eyes riveted on the leadership of the Church. We will not lead you astray. We cannot. This is my witness and my testimony, and my blessing upon you: that the peace of the Lord will be yours now and always; that you'll find it easy all the days of your life to follow the simple, beautiful teachings that are ours in the Book of Mormon, the Doctrine and Covenants, the Pearl of Great Price, and the words of the living prophets. May God grant you the strength and the courage to understand that, and live all the days of your lives by the teachings found in the scriptures. I thank you for who you are and all that you mean to your families and to this Church. You are precious. You are important. You have a great destiny to carry on this glorious work. May you always be worthy, I pray in the name of Jesus Christ. Amen.

Joseph Smith—the Chosen of God and the Friend of Man

Ivan J. Barrett

My beloved brethren and sisters, this is a humbling moment. I have been very much touched and impressed by the singing of this beautiful chorale, by the inspiring and moving prayer by Brother Porter. In fact, coming at the end of the trail, as it were, as far as campus activities are concerned, I seem to have the yearning of the poet, somewhat paraphrased:

Backward, turn backward, oh time, in thy flight.
Make me a freshman again—just for tonight.
[Elisabeth Akers Allen, "Rock Me to Sleep"]

Brothers and sisters, I sincerely pray that the Spirit of the Lord will be with us in rich abundance as it has been thus far, that the things I say may be edifying, uplifting, and worth your coming here this morning.

There was a man who was invited to a masquerade ball. He decided he would go in an unusual costume, so he rented a costume

Ivan J. Barrett was a professor of Church history and doctrine at BYU when this devotional address was given on 12 August 1975. © Brigham Young University.

of the sectarian's idea of the devil. As he walked to the place where the masquerade ball was being held, rain began to fall. He darted into the first open door available along the street, which happened to be the door leading into a church. The minister was in the pulpit, and he was haranguing his audience against that fellow, the evil one. He looked up from his text, and there standing in the doorway in the foyer was the fellow he had been talking against. He immediately made a hurried exit right through the plate-glass window at the back. The audience, wondering why the pastor had made such a hurried exit, looked back and saw the devil standing there in all of his diabolical glee. That particular church was evacuated in record time—all but the heavyset lady who found it difficult to get out of the pew. She finally made her way to the aisle and was trying to hurry to the exit when she fell flat on her face. The devil, gallant fellow that he turned out to be, came over to help her up. As she looked into his diabolical face, fear and consternation written all over hers, she blurted out, "I've been a member of this church for the last thirty years, but I've really been on your side all the time."

As President George A. Smith often said, he knew a lot of Saints in pioneer days that served the Lord like the very devil. The Prophet Joseph Smith taught us how to serve the Lord as the Lord would have us serve him. In fact, he said if we aren't drawing near the Lord in principle, we are going from him and drawing towards the devil.

THE PROPHET'S FRIENDLINESS

There wasn't anything that was so dear to the heart of the Prophet Joseph Smith as friendship. How the Prophet Joseph loved his friends! President Brigham Young said that August day of 1844: "Joseph so loved this people that he gave his life for them. He loved them unto death. You did not know it until after his death" (see *Documentary History of the Church*, 7:240). As the Prophet was leaving Nauvoo to go to Carthage, he stopped before the temple, which was up one story, looked over the city that housed the Saints that he loved, and he exclaimed, "This is the loveliest place and the best people under the heavens; little do they know the trials that await them" (see *Documentary History of the Church*, 6:554).

He could see no fault in the Church. He loved the majority of the Church members so well that he wanted to be resurrected with them. He was not concerned whether they were resurrected in heaven or in hell. In fact, he was to say that if we find ourselves in hell, we will turn the devils out of doors and make a heaven of it. Wherever the Saints should be Joseph knew there would be a good society.

Joseph loved the people. He ended a letter to a new convert in words something like these: "I love your soul and the souls of all men, and do all I can to bring them salvation." The Prophet Joseph Smith taught that "love is one of the chief characteristics of Diety, and ought to be manifested by those who aspire to be the sons of God. A man filled with the love of God, is not content with blessing his family alone, but ranges through the whole world, anxious to bless the whole human race" (*Teachings of the Prophet Joseph Smith*, p. 174). He loved the Saints, but he was not blind to their misgivings or their shortcomings. During the last conference address he gave in mortality, he said, "I love you all; but I hate some of your deeds. I am your best friend, and if persons miss their mark it is their own fault. If I reprove a man, and he hates me, he is a fool; for I love all men, especially these my brethren and sisters" (*Teachings of the Prophet Joseph Smith*, p. 361).

The Prophet was not too concerned as to a man's character if he was his friend. He said, "I will be a friend to him, and preach the Gospel . . . to him, . . . helping him out of his difficulties." Joseph also taught, "Friendship is one of the grand fundamental principles of "Mormonism"; [it is designed] to revolutionize and civilize the world, and cause wars and contentions to cease and men to become friends and brothers" (*Teachings of the Prophet Joseph Smith*, p. 316). The spirit and practice of friendship, my brothers and sisters, is contagious. Said the Prophet Joseph Smith:

It is a time-honored adage that love begets love. Let us pour forth love—show forth our kindness unto all mankind, and the Lord will reward us with

everlasting increase; cast our bread upon the waters and we shall receive
it after many days, increased to a hundredfold. Friendship is like Brother
Turley in his blacksmith shop welding iron to iron; it unites the human fam-
ily with its happy influence. [*Documentary History of the Church,* 5:517]

The spirit of friendship is the essence of charity, which Moroni
defined as the pure love of Christ. Channing Pollock once called love
"friendship put to music" and said, "I thank God for love of life."

Joseph taught, "I do not dwell on your faults, and you shall not
upon mine"—good counsel for us all. He said, "Charity, which is
love, covereth a multitude of sins, and I have covered all the faults
among you, but the prettiest thing in the world is to have not faults
at all. We should cultivate a meek, quiet, and peaceable spirit"
(*Documentary History of the Church,* 5:401).

The Prophet Joseph Smith despised sham. Pretense to him was
folly. Once he said, "I love that man better who swears a stream as
long as my arm, yet deals justice to his neighbors and mercifully deals
his substance to the poor, than the smooth-faced hypocrite. I do not
want you to think that I'm very righteous, for I am not. There was
one good man, and his name was Jesus" (*Documentary History of the
Church,* 5:401).

There came to Nauvoo a Baptist priest to determine the piety of
the Prophet Joseph. When he saw Joseph, he folded his arms and,
weighing his words, uttered, "Is it possible that I now flash my optics
upon a prophet, upon a man who has conversed with my Savior?"

"Yes," said the Prophet, "You've had that privilege. Now, how
would you like to wrestle with me?" (*Journal of Discourses,* 3:67).

THE PROPHET'S FORGIVING NATURE

Joseph Smith's forgiveness of others is impressively illustrated in
an incident involving William W. Phelps. During those trying days of
persecution in Missouri, Phelps apostatized and turned against the
Church. He signed his name to a false affidavit that brought much
suffering to the Saints and imprisoned the Prophet Joseph. In a short

time he realized the error of his ways and asked forgiveness and readmittance into the Church. He wrote the Prophet:

I have seen the folly of my way and tremble at the gulf I have passed. I have done wrong, and I am sorry. The beam is in my own eye. I ask forgiveness in the name of Jesus Christ of all the Saints. For I will do right, God helping me. I want your fellowship, for we are brethren, and our communion used to be sweet. [*Documentary History of the Church*, 4:141–42]

The Prophet's reply reveals the admirable quality of love and forgiveness for the wayward. Wrote the Prophet in reply to William W. Phelp's request to be readmitted into the Church:

I feel a disposition to act on your case in a manner that will meet the approbation of Jehovah, whose servant I am, and inasmuch as long-suffering, patience, and mercy have ever characterized the dealings of our Heavenly Father towards the humble and penitent, I feel disposed to copy that example, cherish the same principles and by so doing be a savior to my fellowman. Believing your confession to be real and your repentance genuine. I shall be happy once again to give you the right hand of fellowship and rejoice over the returning prodigal. Come on, dear brother, since the war is past, for friends at first are friends again at last. [*Documentary History of the Church*, 5:162]

The Prophet Joseph Smith taught, "Ever keep in exercise the principle of mercy and be ready to forgive a brother on the first intimation of repentance and asking forgiveness. And should we even forgive our brother, or even our enemy, before he repents, and asks forgiveness, our Heavenly Father would be equally merciful to us" (*Documentary History of the Church*, 3:383).

Is it any wonder, my brothers and sisters, that Joseph's contemporaries, those who knew him best, were to comment as President Wilford Woodruff did: "When I look at the history of Joseph Smith, I sometimes think that he came as near following the footsteps of the Savior as anyone possibly could" (John A. Widtsoe,

Joseph Smith—Seeker After Truth, p. 348). To bring about peace on the earth and the millennial reign of the Christ, the Prophet Joseph taught that the act of kindness must extend to the animal kingdom. Said he, "Men must become harmless before the brute creation, and when men lost their vicious dispositions and cease to destroy the animal race, the lion and the lamb can dwell together, and the suckling child can play with the serpent in safety" (*Documentary History of the Church*, 2:271). Someone has written:

Be kind to all dumb animals,
And give small birds a crumb;
Be kind to human bein's too,
For they are sometimes dumb.

THE PROPHET'S CORDIAL PERSONALITY

Joseph Smith possessed the secret of making friends. His radiant personality, his acceptance of man's innate goodness, and his love for all men won him many friends. Josiah Quincy was to observe that Joseph was one of the two men, among all he had ever met, who seemed best endowed with that kingly faculty which directs, as by intrinsic right, the feeble and confused souls who are looking for guidance. Parley P. Pratt described Joseph Smith as "possessing a noble boldness, an independence of character. His manner was easy and familiar, his benevolence unbounded as the ocean. Even his most bitter enemies were generally overcome if he could once get their ears" (*Autobiography of Parley P. Pratt*, pp. 45–46).

William Taylor, a brother of President John Taylor, was a personal companion to the Prophet Joseph Smith. These are the words that he said in describing that wonderful man Joseph:

Much has been said of his geniality and his personal magnetism. I was a witness of this. People old or young loved him and trusted him instinctively. I have never known the same joy and satisfaction in the companionship of any other person—man or woman—that I felt with him, the man who conversed with the Almighty. He was always the most companionable and lovable of men, cheerful, and jovial. [*Young Women's Journal*, 17:548]

Dan Jones, a mite of a man physically and a college graduate who left the field of learning to become a sailor, sailed the five oceans and had set foot in almost all of the ports. He ran a steamboat called *The Maid of Iowa* up and down the Mississippi River, and it was seamanship that brought Dan Jones to the Prophet Joseph Smith. One day he landed a boatload of Saints in Nauvoo, and the Prophet came to the wharf to meet him. He walked up to the little captain, put his hand on his shoulder, and said, "God bless this little man." Dan Jones never forgot that benediction. He joined the Church that year to become one of the Prophet's most trusted friends. He was with his beloved Prophet in the Carthage Jail the night before the martyrdom when the Prophet asked, "Brother Jones, are you afraid to die?"

Dan Jones replied, "has it come to that, Brother Joseph? Being engaged in such a work as we're engaged in, I don't think death would have any terror for me."

The Prophet said, "Brother Jones, you shall not die, but you shall go to Wales and fulfill the mission assigned you." After the martyrdom Dan Jones sailed for Wales, where he performed a most successful mission, setting an all-time record for convert baptisms. He testified, "I have come in obedience to the counsel of the martyred prophet, as a messenger to my native land to bear testimony of the work for which his brother Hyrum died, and which he sealed with his own blood." (See Thomas C. Romney, *The Gospel in Action*, p. 89.)

The Prophet Joseph on one occasion was to say, "I'm not an enemy of mankind; I am a friend of mankind. I have no enemies but for the gospel's sake." The Lord promised the Prophet Joseph that he could have anything he desired, and the Prophet was to say, "I have been afraid to ask God to kill my enemies lest some of them, perchance, repent."

During the troublesome days at Far West, Missouri, there came to the home of the Prophet's parents eight men from Daviess County, Missouri, who believed the lies circulated about Joseph Smith and the

Mormons. They had come to kill the Mormon leader. Mother Smith greeted them at the door and invited them to come in. They refused to sit down; in fact, they informed the mother of the Prophet, "We have come to kill him."

Mother Smith was to say, "If you were to see Joseph you would not want to kill him." At that particular point the Prophet Joseph Smith entered the room, and Mother Smith introduced the eight men to him. They stared at him in mute silence. The Prophet smiled, extended his hand, and invited them to be seated. His friendly, cordial manner convinced them that he was guilty neither of murder nor of any other crime. A pleasant half hour was spent, during which time the Prophet explained his views, his feelings, his mission, the purpose of the Church, and the brutal treatment he and the Saints had so unjustly received. He then excused himself, stating that he must be on his way home. Immediately two of the men sprang to their feet and offered to escort him home as they considered it not safe for him to travel alone. He thanked them but did not accept their offer. As the eight men were leaving the house, Mother Smith overheard their departing words. One said, "Did you not feel strange when Smith took you by the hand?"

Another man replied, "I could not move. I would not harm a hair of that man's head for all the world."

The third one said, "I never saw a more harmless, innocent appearing man than the Mormon Prophet."

"Yes, indeed," said the fourth, "that story about him killing those men is a lie, but they'll never fool me again."

THE PROPHET'S LOVE FOR HIS ENEMIES

The Savior, in his inspiring Sermon on the Mount, taught, "Ye have heard that it hath been said, Thou shalt love thy neighbor, and hate thine enemy. But I say unto you, Love your enemies, bless them that curse you, do good to them that hate you, and pray for them which despitefully use you, and persecute you; That ye may be the children of your Father which is in heaven" (Matthew 5:43–45).

The Prophet Joseph Smith practiced this most difficult of all the Savior's teachings. The Prophet was betrayed into the hands of the mob-militia in Missouri. He was court-martialed and sentenced to be shot. One of the officers of the mob-militia, Moses Wilson, came to one of the Prophet's friends, Lyman Wight, and tried to bribe him into testifying against Joseph. He said, "We don't want to kill you, but we have one thing against you, and that is you are too friendly with Joseph Smith. We believe him to be a rascal, but you're a fine fellow. If you will swear against him, we will spare your life and give you any office you want. If you won't you'll be shot at nine o'clock."

Wight looked Wilson squarely in the eye and said, "Wilson, you have your men entirely wrong—both in regard to myself and to Joseph Smith. Joseph Smith is the most philanthropic man I ever saw. He is not your enemy; he is a friend of mankind and a maker of peace. In fact, he is the best friend you have, for if it hadn't been for Joseph Smith, you would have been in hell long ago. I'd have put ya there myself by cuttin' your throat, and Joseph is the only man on earth that could stop me from doin' it. You can just thank Joseph for being alive" (*Documentary History of the Church*, 3:436–37).

Strangely enough, my brothers and sisters, as Parley P. Pratt stated: "If Joseph could get the ears of his most devout enemies he generally made friends of them." Years afterward, Moses Wilson was to say, "Joseph Smith was a most remarkable man. I carried him a prisoner in chains to my house in Independence, Missouri, and he hadn't been there two hours before my wife loved him better than she loved me."

After being kidnapped by two sheriffs and brutally treated by them, his life constantly being threatened, the Prophet Joseph was rescued by his friends. Instead of his being escorted across the Mississippi River into Missouri, as the sheriffs intended to do, he was brought to Nauvoo. While in Nauvoo, the prophet took the two sheriffs to his home, placed them at the head of his table, and his wife waited on them as though they were the most honored guests that had ever graced her house. Joseph said, "I have brought these men to Nauvoo, not as prisoners in chains, but as prisoners of kindness.

I have treated them kindly. I have had the privilege of returning them good for evil" (*Documentary History of the Church*, 5:467).

The Prophet Joseph Smith was quick to express his gratitude for any little act of kindness or gift given him. In fact, he was to say that ingratitude was one of the most offensive sins of his age. On one occasion his friends gave him $64.50, and this is what the Prophet Joseph said: "My heart swells with gratitude inexpressible when I realize the great condescension of my Heavenly Father in opening the hearts of these, my beloved brethren, to administer so liberally to my wants."

While in the Liberty Jail he received letters from his wife, Emma, and other friends which certainly gave him courage to face the loneliness of imprisonment for Christ's sake. Then he wrote, "One token of friendship from any source whatever awakens and calls into action every sympathetic feeling." The Lord assured his Prophet while in the Liberty Jail, "Thy friends do stand by thee, and they shall hail thee again with warm hearts and friendly hands" (D&C 121:9).

When the enemies of the Prophet Joseph were seeking his life during the Nauvoo period, the Prophet was forced to go into hiding, and on one occasion some of his friends visited him. After their departure he wrote, "How good and glorious it has seemed unto me to find pure and holy friends who are faithful, just, and true, and whose hearts fail them not and whose knees are confirmed and do not falter. These I have met in prosperity, and they were my friends, and now I meet them in adversity, and they are still my warmer friends" (*Documentary History of the Church*, 5:107). The Prophet Joseph sums up most impressively why they were his friends:

[First and foremost] *these love the God that I serve;* [secondly] *they love the truths that I promulgate;* [thirdly] *they love those virtuous, and those holy doctrines that I cherish in my bosom with the warmest feelings of my heart. I love friendship and truth; I love virtue and law; I love the God of Abraham, of Isaac, and of Jacob; and they are my brethren, and I shall live; and because I live they shall live also.* [*Documentary History of the Church,* 5:108–9]

As he prayed for his friends, the still, small voice whispered to his soul, "These, that share your toils with such faithful hearts, shall reign with you in the kingdom of their God" (*Documentary History of the Church*, 5:109). What a glorious reward of friendship! What wouldn't one of us give to have the privilege of being with the Prophet Joseph Smith in the kingdom of God?

THE PRINCIPLE OF LOVE

While conversing with his cousin George A. Smith on one occasion, the Prophet wrapped his arms around him and said with emotion, "George A., I love you as I love my own soul!" This left his cousin speechless. In fact, George A. said, "I felt so affected I could hardly speak." In a few moments, after regaining his composure, he solemnly said, "I hope, Brother Joseph, that my whole life and actions will prove my feelings and the depth of my affection for you" (*Documentary History of the Church*, 5:39).

Sectarian priests often asked concerning Joseph, "How can this babbler get so many followers around him and retain them?" The Prophet answered, "It's because I possess the principle of love. All I have to offer the world is a good heart and a good hand" (*Teachings of the Prophet Joseph Smith*, p. 313). Joseph's love and concern for his brethren was shown in action. Word came to Nauvoo on one occasion of a poor man who had lost his house by fire. Nearly all the brethren said they were sorry for the man. The Prophet Joseph Smith put his hand in his pocket and pulled out a five-dollar gold piece and said, "I feel sorry for this brother to the amount of five dollars. How much do you feel sorry?"

Phineas H. Young, an older brother of the Prophet Brigham Young, was once away in Tiffin, Ohio. While there he wrote Willard Richards, the Prophet Joseph's secretary, and said, "I long to see the day when I can again visit my brethren and see the Lord's Prophet, and hear the words of life sweetly distilling from his lips. Give my love to Brother Joseph when you see him. Tell him I'd come to the Rocky Mountains to see him and fight my way through an army of wildcats and Missouri wolves and live on skunks the whole journey" ("Journal History of the Church," 14 December 1842).

Well, meeting the Prophet Joseph was an experience, my friends, and those who had had that opportunity never forgot. Amos M. Lyman traveled some six hundred miles to see the Prophet Joseph Smith. He was the only member of his family to join the Church. He arrived at the John Johnson home in Hiram, Ohio, and received employment working on the farm for ten dollars a month. Shortly after his coming, the prophet Joseph returned from Missouri, and young Lyman had the opportunity of meeting him. The impression the Prophet made on the new convert was stamped indelibly upon his mind, heart, and soul through the years: "When he grasped me by the hand in that cordial way, known to those who had met him in the honest simplicity of truth, I felt as one of old in the presence of the Lord, my strength seemed to be gone so that it required an effort on my part to stand on my feet; but in all of this there was no fear, but the serenity and peace of heaven pervaded my soul and the still small voice of the Spirit whispered its living testimony in the depths of my soul, where it has ever remained, that he was a man of God" (*Deseret News*, 8:117).

Now, the climax of all the teachings of the Prophet Joseph Smith on love and friendship: "Until we have obtained perfect love we are liable to fall, and when we have the testimony that our names are sealed in the Lamb's Book of Life we have perfect love, and then it isn't possible for false Christs to deceive us" (*Teachings of the Prophet Joseph Smith*, p. 9).

One of the most touching scenes in the life of the Prophet Joseph (and one of the most thrilling, for it demonstrates the unbounded love of his followers for their beloved Prophet) was when, in the summer of 1843, the Prophet Joseph Smith rode triumphantly into Nauvoo after he had been kidnapped by a couple of sheriffs. His friends had come to the rescue, and he entered Nauvoo in triumph. The Saints had been notified the day before of his coming, and almost all the people came out meet him, with his wife, Emma, and his brother, Hyrum in the lead. After embracing his wife and his brother Hyrum, he mounted his favorite horse, Old Charlie. The band struck up "Hail, Columbia," and the procession started into town. Besides a long line of carriages and persons on horseback, the streets were lined with people whose countenances were joyous and full of satisfaction to see their beloved Prophet once more safe. The Prophet was greeted with cheers from the people and the booming of gun and cannon.

At his home he was embraced by his mother, with tears of joy streaming down her cheeks, while his little children clung to him with feelings of enthusiastic and enraptured pleasure. His little son Fred exclaimed, "Pa, the Missourians won't take you away again, will they?" His friends from out of town looked on with amazement and astonishment, but with unconcealed pleasure at the loving attachment of the Prophet's family and his friends toward him. His friends were loath to depart. One can feel the Prophet's love for his friends as he blessed them: "I thank you for your kindness and love for me. I bless you all, in the name of Jesus Christ."

Josiah Quincy spent two days in Nauvoo. He followed the Prophet Joseph around. He noted the power and influence of the Prophet as he walked among the people. It was then that Quincy said, "General Smith, it seems to me that you have too much power to be safely trusted in one man."

Joseph replied, "In your hands, or that of any other man, so much power would no doubt be dangerous. I am the only man in the world whom it would be safe to trust with it. Remember, I am a prophet." And in all the solemnity of my soul I testify to you that he is and was a prophet, a servant of the Most High God, a seer of God, a revealer of truth, and a friend to man, in the sacred name of our Lord Jesus Christ. Amen.

The Profile of a Prophet

Hugh B. Brown

I should like to dispense with all formality, if I may, and address
both faculty and students as my brothers and sisters. I adopt that
form of salutation for several reasons: first, practically all who are
here are members of the Church that established and maintains this
university; second, I believe in the fatherhood of God and the broth-
erhood of man; and third, I do not intend to give a lecture, certainly
not an oration or even a sermon, but simply wish to bear my testimony to my brothers and sisters.

I should like to be for a few minutes a witness in support of
the proposition that the gospel of Jesus Christ has been restored in
our day and that this is His Church, organized under His direction
through the Prophet Joseph Smith. I should like to give some reasons
for the faith I have and for my allegiance to the Church.

Perhaps I can do this more quickly by referring to an interview
I had in London, England, in 1939, just before the outbreak of the
war. I had met a very prominent English gentleman, a member of the

*Hugh B. Brown was assistant to the Quorum of the Twelve Apostles of The Church
of Jesus Christ of Latter-day Saints when this devotional address was delivered at
Brigham Young University on 4 October 1955.* © *Intellectual Reserve, Inc.*

House of Commons, formerly one of the justices of the supreme court
of England. In my conversations with this gentleman on various subjects—"vexations of the soul," he called them—we talked about business, law, politics, international relations, and war, and we frequently
discussed religion.

He called me on the phone one day and asked if I would meet
him at his office and explain some phases of the gospel. He said,
"I think there is going to be a war. If there is, you will have to return
to America and we may not meet again." His statement regarding the
imminence of war and the possibility that we would not meet again
proved to be prophetic.

When I went to his office he said he was intrigued by some things
I had told him. He asked me to prepare a brief on Mormonism.

I may say to you students that a brief is a statement of law and
facts that lawyers like President Wilkinson prepare when they are
going into court to argue a case.

He asked me to prepare a brief on Mormonism and discuss it
with him as I would discuss a legal problem. He said, "You have told
me that you believe that Joseph Smith was a prophet. You have said
to me that you believe that God the Father and Jesus of Nazareth
appeared to Joseph Smith. I cannot understand how a barrister and
solicitor from Canada, a man trained in logic and evidence, could
accept such absurd statements. What you tell me about Joseph Smith
seems fantastic, but I think you should take three days at least to prepare a brief and permit me to examine it and question you on it."

I suggested that we proceed at once and have an examination
for discovery, which is, briefly, a meeting of the opposing sides in a
lawsuit where the plaintiff and defendant, with their attorneys, meet
to examine each other's claims and see if they can find some area of
agreement, thus saving the time of the court later on.

I said perhaps we could see whether we had some common
ground from which we could discuss my "fantastic ideas." He agreed
to that quite readily.

I can only give you, in the few minutes at my disposal, a
condensed and abbreviated synopsis of the three-hour conversation

that followed. In the interest of time I shall resort to the question-and-answer method, rather than narration.

I began by asking, "May I proceed, sir, on the assumption that you are a Christian?"

"I am."

"I assume you believe in the Bible—the Old and New Testaments?"

"I do!"

"Do you believe in prayer?"

"I do!"

"You say that my belief that God spoke to a man in this age is fantastic and absurd?"

"To me it is."

"Do you believe that God ever did speak to anyone?"

"Certainly, all through the Bible we have evidence of that."

"Did He speak to Adam?"

"Yes."

"To Enoch, Noah, Abraham, Moses, Jacob, Joseph, and on through the prophets?"

"I believe He spoke to each of them."

"Do you believe that contact between God and man ceased when Jesus appeared on the earth?"

"No, such communication reached its climax, its apex, at that time."

"Do you believe that Jesus was the Son of God?"

"He was."

"Do you believe, sir, that after Jesus was resurrected, a certain lawyer—who was also a tentmaker by the name of Saul of Tarsus—when on his way to Damascus talked with Jesus of Nazareth, who had been crucified, resurrected, and had ascended into heaven?"

"I do."

"Whose voice did Saul hear?"

"It was the voice of Jesus Christ, for He so introduced Himself."

"Then, my Lord—that is the way we address judges in the British Commonwealth—I am submitting to you in all seriousness that it was standard procedure in Bible times for God to talk to man."

"I think I will admit that, but it stopped shortly after the first century of the Christian era."

"Why do you think it stopped?"

"I can't say."

"You think that God hasn't spoken since then?"

"I am sure He hasn't."

"There must be a reason. Can you give me a reason?"

"I do not know."

"May I suggest some possible reasons? Perhaps God does not speak to man anymore because He cannot. He has lost the power."

He said, "Of course that would be blasphemous."

"Well, then, if you don't accept that, perhaps He doesn't speak to men because He doesn't love us anymore and He is no longer interested in the affairs of men."

"No," he said, "God loves all men, and He is no respecter of persons."

"Well, then, if He could speak, and if He loves us, then the only other possible answer, as I see it, is that we don't need Him. We have made such rapid strides in science and we are so well educated that we don't need God anymore."

And then he said—and his voice trembled as he thought of impending war—"Mr. Brown, there never was a time in the history of the world when the voice of God was needed as it is needed now. Perhaps you can tell me why He doesn't speak."

My answer was: "He *does* speak, He has spoken; but men need faith to hear Him."

Then we proceeded to prepare what I may call a "profile of a prophet."

Perhaps you students would like to amplify what I must condense today and draw your own standard or definition of a prophet and see whether Joseph Smith measures up.

We agreed between us that the following characteristics should distinguish a man who claims to be a prophet:

1. He will boldly claim that God had spoken to him.

2. Any man so claiming would be a dignified man with a dignified message—no table jumping, no whisperings from the dead, no clairvoyance, but an intelligent statement of truth.

3. Any man claiming to be a prophet of God would declare his message without any fear and without making any weak concessions to public opinion.

4. If he were speaking for God he could not make concessions, although what he taught would be new and contrary to the accepted teachings of the day. A prophet bears witness to what he has seen and heard and seldom tries to make a case by argument. His message and not himself is important.

5. Such a man would speak in the name of the Lord, saying, "Thus said the Lord," as did Moses, Joshua, and others.

6. Such a man would predict future events in the name of the Lord, and they would come to pass, as did those predicted by Isaiah and Ezekiel.

7. He would have not only an important message for his time but often a message for all future time, such as Daniel, Jeremiah, and others had.

8. He would have courage and faith enough to endure persecution and to give his life, if need be, for the cause he espoused, such as Peter, James, Paul, and others did.

9. Such a man would denounce wickedness fearlessly. He would generally be rejected or persecuted by the people of his time, but later generations and descendants of his persecutors would build monuments in his honor.

10. He would be able to do superhuman things—things that no man could do without God's help. The consequence or result of his message and work would be convincing evidence of his prophetic calling: "By their fruits ye shall know them" (Matthew 7:20).

11. His teachings would be in strict conformity with scripture, and his words and his writings would become scripture. "For the

prophecy came not in old time by the will of man: but holy men of God spake as they were moved by the Holy Ghost" (2 Peter 1:21).

Now I have given but an outline that you can fill in and amplify and then measure and judge the Prophet Joseph Smith by the work and stature of other prophets.

As a student of the life of the Prophet Joseph Smith for more than 50 years, I say to you young men and women: by these standards Joseph Smith qualifies as a prophet of God.

I believe that Joseph Smith was a prophet of God because he talked like a prophet. He was the first man since the apostles of Jesus Christ were slain to make the claim that prophets have always made—viz., that God had spoken to him. He lived and died like a prophet. I believe he was a prophet of God because he gave to this world some of the greatest of all revelations. I believe that he was a prophet of God because he predicted many things that have come to pass—things that only God could bring to pass.

John, the beloved disciple of Jesus, declared, "The testimony of Jesus is the spirit of prophecy" (Revelation 19:10). If Joseph Smith had the testimony of Jesus, he had the spirit of prophecy. And if he had the spirit of prophecy, he was a prophet.

I submit to you, and I submitted to my friend, that as much as any man who ever lived, he had a testimony of Jesus, for, like the apostles of old, he saw Him and heard Him speak. He gave his life for that testimony. I challenge any man to name one who has given more evidence of the divine calling of Jesus Christ than did the Prophet Joseph Smith.

I believe the Prophet Joseph Smith was a prophet because he did many superhuman things. One was translating the Book of Mormon. Some people will not agree, but I submit to you that the Prophet Joseph Smith in translating the Book of Mormon did a superhuman work. I ask you students to undertake to write a story on the ancient inhabitants of America, to write as he did without any source of material. Include in your story 54 chapters dealing with wars, 21 historical chapters, and 55 chapters on visions and prophecies. And, remember, when you begin to write on visions and prophecies, you must have your record agree meticulously with the Bible. You must write 71 chapters on doctrine and exhortation, and here, too, you must check every statement with the scriptures or you will be proven to be a fraud. You must write 21 chapters on the ministry of Christ, and everything you claim He said and did and every testimony you write in your book about Him must agree absolutely with the New Testament.

I ask you, would you like to undertake such a task? I would suggest to you too that you must employ figures of speech, similes, metaphors, narrations, exposition, description, oratory, epic, lyric, logic, and parables. Undertake that, will you?

I ask you to remember that the man who translated the Book of Mormon was a young man who hadn't had the opportunity of schooling that you have had, and yet he dictated that book in just a little over two months and made very few, if any, corrections. For over one hundred years some of the best students and scholars of the world have been trying to prove from the Bible that the Book of Mormon is false, but not one of them has been able to prove that anything he wrote was not in strict harmony with the scriptures—with the Bible and with the word of God.

The Book of Mormon not only declares on the title page that its purpose is to convince Jew and Gentile that Jesus is the Christ, the Eternal God, but this truth is the burden of its message. In 3 Nephi it is recorded that multitudes of people testified, "We saw Him. We felt of His hands and His side. We know He is the Christ" (see 3 Nephi 11:14–15).

Joseph Smith undertook and accomplished other superhuman tasks. Among them I list the following:

He organized the Church. (I call attention to the fact that no constitution effected by human agency has survived 100 years without modification or amendment, even the Constitution of the United States. The basic law or constitution of the Church has never been altered.)

He undertook to carry the gospel message to all nations, which is a superhuman task still in progress.

He undertook, by divine command, to gather thousands of people to Zion.

He instituted vicarious work for the dead and built temples for that purpose.

He promised that certain signs should follow the believers, and there are thousands of witnesses who certify that this promise has been fulfilled.

I said to my friend, "My Lord, I cannot understand your saying to me that my claims are fantastic. Nor can I understand why Christians who claim to believe in Christ would persecute and put to death a man whose whole purpose was to prove the truth of the things they themselves were declaring; namely, that Jesus was the Christ. I could understand their persecuting Joseph if he had said, 'I am Christ,' or if he had said, 'There is no Christ,' or if he had said someone else is Christ. Then Christians believing in Christ would be justified in opposing him.

"But what he said was, 'He whom ye claim to serve, declare I unto you,' paraphrasing what Paul said in Athens: 'Whom therefore ye ignorantly worship, him declare I unto you' (Acts 17:23). Joseph said to the Christians of his day, 'You claim to believe in Jesus Christ. I testify that I saw Him and I talked with Him. He is the Son of God. Why persecute me for that?'

"When Joseph came out of the woods, he had at least four fundamental truths, and he announced them to the world: first, that the Father and the Son are separate and distinct individuals; second, that the canon of scripture is not complete; third, that man was created in the bodily image of God; and fourth, the channel between earth and heaven is open and revelation is continuous."

Perhaps some of you are wondering how the judge reacted to our discussion. He listened intently; he asked some very pointed and searching questions; and, at the end of the period, he said, "Mr. Brown, I wonder if your people appreciate the import of your message. Do you?" He said, "If what you have told me is true, it is the greatest message that has come to this earth since the angels announced the birth of Christ."

This was a judge speaking—a great statesman, an intelligent man. He threw out the challenge: "Do you appreciate the import of what you say?" He added, "I wish it were true. I hope it may be true. God knows it ought to be true. I would to God," he said, and he wept as he said it, "that some man could appear on earth and authoritatively say, 'Thus saith the Lord.'"

As I intimated, we did not meet again. I have brought to you very briefly some of the reasons why I believe that Joseph Smith was a prophet of God. But undergirding and overarching all that, I say to you from the very center of my heart that by the revelations of the Holy Ghost I know that Joseph Smith was a prophet of God.

Although these evidences and many others that could be cited may have the effect of giving one an intellectual conviction, only by the whisperings of the Holy Spirit can one come to know the things of God. By those whisperings I say I know that Joseph Smith is a prophet of God. I thank God for that knowledge and pray for His blessings upon all of you in the name of Jesus Christ, amen.

"Joseph Smith, the Mormon Prophet"

James A. Cullimore

My young brethren and sisters of this great school, I am delighted to greet you this very first day you're back to school from your holidays. I hope you all had a wonderful Christmas and are on the road to a successful and happy New Year.

This is such a special time of the year—this holiday—Christmas and New Year. I trust we have been greatly blessed by the spirit of Christmas and the Christ child and that we may have that spirit to be with us and bless us in our lives all the year.

It would be interesting to know what your resolutions are in the New Year; and although one should not wait until the New Year to repent, it does furnish a good time to make a change. I like these verses in reference to the New Year.

A Clean New Book
Midnight strikes, and the old year is gone.
We close the tablets we've written on:
And, torn 'twixt hope and doubt and fear,
We open the book of an unlived year.

James A. Cullimore was a member of the First Quorum of the Seventy of The Church of Jesus Christ of Latter-day Saints when this devotional address was given at Brigham Young University on 4 January 1977. © *Intellectual Reserve, Inc.*

An unlived year. Ah, stained with tears
Are the well-thumbed volumes of other years.
Soiled by blunders and black regret
Are the pages we read with our eyelids—wet.

Close in our hearts, as the leaves are turned
Is the record of passions that flared and burned;
And panics and sorrow, and ghosts that leer,
Look out from the page of the dying year.

But fresh in our hands—once more—is laid
A clean new book, by the Master made;
Unmarred are the pages lying there
Twelve new chapters, fresh and fair.

It is ours to write the daily tale
Of how we conquer or how we fail;
Of struggle and effort and hope that wakes
Like a sun in the heart when a bright day breaks.

Once a year, when the glad bells ring,
And the old year nods to a baby King,
Fresh in our hands, with the title clear
And the leaves uncut, is an unlived year. [Author Unknown]

Florence French wrote these verses:

I would like to change the picture
I painted yesterday;
The harsh tones would be muted,
The background be less gray.

The leafless trees of winter
Would take on tints of spring;
The silent, ice-bound river
Would be a sparkling thing.

The scarlet tanager would replace
The starling's somber shade;
The pink of wild rose fill the space
Where drifting leaves pervade.

I cannot change the picture
I painted yesterday,
But I can make a new one—
And I'll begin today.

A man who had been in the penitentiary applied to Henry Ford for employment. He had decided to tell Mr. Ford about his past as he applied. He had not been honest on several occasions as he had applied and after he was hired and working, his employer had found out he had been in the penitentiary and let him go. So now as he started to tell about his past, Mr. Ford stopped him and said, "I don't care about your past; start where you stand."

Berton Braley put these thoughts to verse:

Start where you stand and never mind the past;
The past won't help you in beginning new;
If you have left it all behind at last
Why, that's enough, you've done with it, you're through; . . .

Forget the buried woes and dead despairs;
Here is a brand-new trial right at hand;
The future is for him who does and dares;
Start where you stand. . . .

What has been, has been; yesterday is dead
And by it you are neither blessed nor banned;
Take courage, man, be brave and drive ahead;
Start where you stand.

Repentance is one of the greatest principles of the gospel.

There is another important event that is often lost track of in the busy holiday season, or only little is made of it. I refer to the birthday of the Prophet Joseph Smith on December 23. As members of The Church of Jesus Christ of Latter-day Saints, we recognize Joseph Smith as a prophet of God through whom the Church was restored in this dispensation. No one is more revered by us save Jesus Christ himself. Even though we revere him as our Prophet and the founder of the Church, it is unlikely that we fully comprehend his true greatness. May I share with you a few of the attributes and virtues that made him one of the greatest men ever to live upon the earth.

John Henry Evans wrote of him:

Here is a man who was born in the stark hills of Vermont; who was reared in the backwoods of New York; who never looked inside a college or a high school; who lived in six States, no one of which would own him during his lifetime; who spent months in the vile prisons of the period; who, even when he had his freedom, was hounded like a fugitive; who was covered once with a coat of tar and feathers, and left for dead; who, with his following, was driven by irate neighbors from New York to Ohio, from Ohio to Missouri, and from Missouri to Illinois; and who, at the unripe age of thirty-eight, was shot to death by a mob with painted faces.

Yet this man became mayor of the biggest town in Illinois and the state's most prominent citizen, the commander of the largest body of trained soldiers in the nation outside the Federal army, the founder of cities and of a university, and aspired to become President of the United States.

He wrote a book which has baffled the literary critics for a hundred years and which is today more widely read than any other volume save the Bible. On the threshold of an organizing age he established the most nearly perfect social mechanism in the modern world, and developed a religious philosophy that challenges anything of the kind in history, for completeness and cohesion. And he set up the machinery for an economic system that would take the brood of Fears out of the heart of man—the fear of want through sickness, old age, unemployment, and poverty.

In thirty nations are men and women who look upon him as a greater leader than Moses and a greater prophet than Isaiah; his disciples now number close to a million; and already a granite shaft pierces the sky over the place where he was born, and another is in course of erection over the place where he received the inspiration for his Book. [John Henry Evans, *Joseph Smith, An American Prophet,* p. v]

Joseph Smith occupies a unique place among the prophets—his birth and his name, Joseph, were known nearly four thousand years before he came to the earth. Joseph who was sold into Egypt said of the great latter-day prophet:

"Yea, Joseph truly said: Thus saith the lord unto me; a choice seer will I raise up. . . .

". . . Behold; that seer will the Lord bless. . . .

"And his name shall be called after me; and it shall be after the name of his father. And he shall be like unto me; for the thing, which the Lord shall bring forth by this hand, but the power of the Lord shall bring my people unto salvation.

"Yea, thus prophesied Joseph: I am sure of this thing. . . ." (2 Nephi 3:7, 14–16).

Not only was the Prophet Joseph's birth known, but after his death, the Lord caused to have written and included as scripture the following:

"Joseph Smith, the Prophet and Seer of the Lord, has done more, save Jesus only, for the salvation of men in this world, than any other man that ever lived in it. . . ." [Leon Hartshorn, *Classic Stories from the Lives of Our Prophets,* p. 1]

He lived great, and he died great in the eyes of God and his people; and like most of the Lord's anointed in ancient times, has sealed his mission and his works with his own blood . . . [D&C 135:3]

Dr. John A. Widtsoe said of the Prophet Joseph:

Since I struggled as a boy to find the Church and the message of Joseph Smith I have been overwhelmed by the greatness of the Prophet. He towers above all men by his great teachings.

Of course he was a man with the frailties of the flesh, but he so lived that God spoke to men through him. Indeed, he is the biggest man in the history of the world since the Savior lived among men nearly two thousand years ago. He was a magnificent type of man.

The Prophet stands unique among the religious leaders of the world, for in practically all of his work in the restoration he had witnesses. Mohammed, Buddha, Confucius, as examples, each established his work without witnesses, but not so Joseph Smith.

There were witnesses to the Gold Plates and the Book of Mormon, in the visitation of heavenly personages, and in the receiving of many of the revelations. His work was inaugurated not by himself alone, but by and with witnesses.

His teachings clear up so many misconceptions, that any man who honestly investigates the Prophet and his work, must come to a conviction that he was indeed a Prophet. [Church Section, *Deseret News*, January 30, 1952, p. 3]

Possibly few tributes have been given of the Prophet greater than that of Josiah Quincy in his *Figures of the Past.*

It is by no means improbable that some future text-book, for the use of generations yet unborn, will contain a questions something like this: What historical American of the nineteenth century has exerted the most power-ful influence upon the destinies of his countrymen? And it is by no means impossible that the answer to that interrogatory may be thus written: Joseph Smith, the Mormon Prophet. And the reply, absurd as it doubtless seems to most men now living, may be an obvious commonplace to their descendants. History deals in surprises and para doxes quite as startling as this. The man who established a religion in this age of free debate, who was and is today accepted by hundreds of thousands as a direct emissary from the Most High,—such a rare human being is not to be disposed of by pelting his memory with unsavory epithets. [Josiah Quincy, *Figures of the Past*, p. 376]

A Russian historian once visited the United States for something over a year studying the history of great Americans and American institutions. As he was about to board his ship to return to his native land, newspapermen interrogated him. One of them asked him this question: "In your study of great Americans during this past year, which of them do you consider to be the greatest?" His answer is most startling. He said, "You have only had one truly great American, one man who gave to the world ideas that could change the whole destiny of the human race—Joseph Smith, the Mormon prophet."

The Prophet was tried and tested and suffered many indignities. He was falsely arrested 42 times but was always cleared by the law of the land. He was tarred and feathered. He spent nearly six months in Liberty Jail in terrible conditions and with food not fit for humans. Parley P. Pratt says of one of these occasions:

In one of those tedious nights we had lain as if in sleep till the hour of midnight had passed, and our ears and hearts had been pained, while we had listened for hours to the obscene jests, the horrid oaths, the dreadful blasphemies and filthy language of our guards, Colonel Price at their head, as they recounted to each other their deeds of rapine, murder, robbery, etc., which they had committed among the "Mormons" while at Far West and vicinity. They even boasted of defiling by force wives, daughters and virgins, and of shooting or dashing out the brains of men, women and children.

I had listened till I became so disgusted, shocked, horrified, and so filled with the spirit of indignant justice that I could scarcely refrain from rising upon my feet and rebuking the guards; but had said nothing to Joseph, or any one else, although I lay next to him and knew he was awake. On a sudden he arose to his feet, and spoke in a voice of thunder, or as the roaring lion, uttering, as near as I can recollect, the following words:

"SILENCE, ye fiends of the infernal pit. In the name of Jesus Christ I rebuke you, and command you to be still; I will not live another minute and hear such language. Cease such talk, or you or I die THIS INSTANT!"

He ceased to speak. He stood erect in terrible majesty. Chained, and without a weapon; calm, unruffled and dignified as an angel, he looked upon the quailing guards, whose weapons were lowered or dropped to the ground; whose knees smote together, and who, shrinking into a corner or crouching at his feet, begged his pardon, and remained quiet till a change of guards.

I have seen the ministers of justice, clothed in magisterial robes, and criminals arraigned before them, while life was suspended on a breath, in the Courts of England; I have witnessed a Congress in solemn session to give laws to nations; I have tried to conceive of kings of royal courts, of thrones and crowns; and of emperors assembled to decide the fate of kingdoms; but dignity and majesty have I seen but once, *as it stood in chains, at midnight, in a dungeon in an obscure village of Missouri. [Autobiography of Parley P. Pratt,* pp. 210–211]

One of the tests of a true prophet is whether his prophecies come true.

Elder John A. Widtsoe in his book, "Joseph Smith the Prophet," makes an interesting statement about the prophecies of Joseph Smith. He says: "From the revelations printed in the Doctrine and Covenants are found 1,100 statements that may be classed as prophecies of the future. Nearly 700 are of a spiritual nature; the other 400 deal directly with the things of the earth."

I will mention only five of his well-known prophecies to which we've all made reference time and again. He predicted that three witnesses should see the golden plates and should testify of their experience. He prophesied to Stephen A. Douglas in 1843 that the time would come when he, Stephen A. Douglas, would aspire to the presidency of the United States, but that if he ever turned his hand against the Latter-day Saints he would feel the weight of Almighty God upon him. The rest is history. Douglas did turn his hands against the saints, he went down to political defeat and died an embittered man.

In 1832 the Prophet Joseph Smith prophesied that war would shortly come to pass, beginning in the rebellion of South Carolina and that the Southern States would be divided against the Northern States, etc. He prophesied in that same revelation that the time would come when war would be poured out upon all nations. World War One and World War Two and what has followed after have been a vindication of his place as a foreteller of events. In 1842 he prophesied that the saints would be driven to the Rocky Mountains and some would assist in making settlements and building cities and see the saints become a mighty people in the midst of the Rocky Mountains.

But beyond being merely a foreteller of future events, what is it that characterizes a true Prophet of God? First he is God's mouthpiece of that day and to his group. Second, he restates the ancient truths, and seeks to hold the people to unchanging laws of the gospel. Third, he receives additional revelations from the Lord to meet the problems of the progressive unfolding plan. Such new truths emanating from Deity come only through the Prophet of the day. Such a man was Joseph Smith, in every sense a Prophet of God. Yes, truly as Prophet Amos has said, "Surely the Lord God will do nothing save He revealeth His secrets unto His servants the Prophets." [Church News, *Deseret News*, December 10, 1955, p. 13]

Miracles as great as those in the meridian dispensation were accomplished by Joseph Smith during his life. President Wilford Woodruff gives an account of some of these healings.

While I was living in this cabin in the old barracks, we experienced a day of God's power with the Prophet Joseph. It was a very sickly time and Joseph had given up his home in Commerce to the sick, and had a tent pitched in his door-yard and was living in that himself. The large number of Saints who had been driven out of Missouri, were flocking into Commerce; but had no homes to go into, and were living in wagons, in tents, and on the ground. Many, therefore, were sick through the exposure they were subjected to. Brother Joseph had waited on the sick, until he was worn out and nearly sick himself.

On the morning of the 22nd of July, 1839, he arose reflecting upon the situation of the Saints of God in their persecutions and afflictions, and he called upon the Lord in prayer, and the power of God rested upon him mightily, and as Jesus healed all the sick around Him in His day, so Joseph, the Prophet of God, healed all around on this occasion. He healed all in his house and door-yard, then, in company with Sidney Rigdon and several of the Twelve, he went through among the sick lying on the bank of the river, and he commanded them in a loud voice, in the name of Jesus Christ, to come up and be made whole, and they were all healed. When he healed all that were sick on the east side of the river, they crossed the Mississippi river in a ferry-boat to the west side, to Montrose, where we were. The first house they went into was President Brigham Young's. He was sick on his bed at the time. The Prophet went into his house and healed him, and they all came out together. As they were passing by my door, Brother Joseph said: "Brother Woodruff, follow me." These were the only words spoken by any of the company from the time they left Brother Brigham's till we crossed the public square, and entered Brother [Elijah] Fordham's house. Brother Fordham had been dying for an hour, and we expected each minute would be his last.

I felt the power of God that was overwhelming His Prophet.

When we entered the house, Brother Joseph walked up to Brother Fordham, and took him by the right hand; and in his left hand he held his hat.

He saw that Brother Fordham's eyes were glazed, and that he was speechless and unconscious.

After taking hold of his hand, he looked down into the dying man's face and said: "Brother Fordham, do you not know me?" At first he made no reply; but we could all see the effect of the Spirit of God resting upon him.

He again said: "Elijah, do you not know me?"

With a low whisper, Brother Fordham answered, "Yes!"

The Prophet then said, "Have you faith to be healed?"

The answer, which was a little plainer than before, was: "I am afraid it is too late. If you had come sooner, I think it might have been."

He had the appearance of a man waking from sleep. It was the sleep of death.

Joseph then said: "Do you believe that Jesus is the Christ?"

"I do, Brother Joseph," was the response.

Then the Prophet of God spoke with a loud voice, as in the majesty of the Godhead: "Elijah, I command you, in the name of Jesus of Nazareth, to arise and be made whole!"

The words of the Prophet were not like the words of man, but like the voice of God. It seemed to me that the house shook from its foundation.

Elijah Fordham leaped from his bed like a man raised from the dead. A healthy color came to his face, and life was manifested in every act.

His feet were done up in Indian meal poultices. He kicked them off his feet, . . . and then called for his clothes and put them on. He asked for a bowl of bread and milk, and ate it; then put on his hat and followed us into the street to visit others who were sick. . . .

As soon as we left Brother Fordham's house, we went into the house of Brother Joseph B. Noble. Who was very low and dangerously sick.

When we entered the house, Brother Joseph took him by the hand, and commanded him, in the name of Jesus Christ, to arise and be made whole. He did arise and was immediately healed. . . .

While waiting for the ferry-boat, a man of the world, knowing of the miracles performed, came to him and asked him if he would not go and heal two twin children of his, about five months old, who were both lying sick nigh unto death.

They were some two miles from Montrose.

The Prophet said he could not go; but, after pausing some time, he said he would send some one to heal them; and he turned to me and said: "You go with the man and heal his children."

He took a red silk handkerchief out of his pocket and gave it to me, and told me to wipe their faces with the handkerchief when I administered to them, and they should be healed. He also said unto me: "As long as you will keep that handkerchief, it shall remain a league between you and me."

I went with the man, and did as the Prophet commanded me, and the children were healed.

I have possession of the handkerchief unto this day. [Wilford Woodruff, *Leaves from my Journal,* pp. 62–65]

Few men have been privileged to see God the Father and Christ while in mortal life as did the Prophet Joseph Smith. Few have been so honored with the many manifestations as he was. Quoting President George Albert Smith, President Harold B. Lee said of the Prophet Joseph in a general conference of the Church: "'. . . Many have belittled Joseph Smith, but those who have will be forgotten in the remains of mother earth, and . . . their infamy will ever be with them, but honor, majesty, and fidelity to God, exemplified by Joseph

Smith and attached to his name, will never die'" (*Conference Report,* October 7, 1973, p. 166).

There are those who would say, I can accept everything in the Church except that Joseph Smith is a prophet of God; or, I can belong to your church if you would do away with the principle of continued revelation. It is difficult for me to understand how one could accept the gospel without accepting him who was the instrument in its restoration, or reject the principle of continued revelation, upon which the Church is founded. It is important that each of us come to know for ourselves, individually, that Joseph Smith was and is a prophet of God, that he did see God and Christ, and was an instrument in the establishment of the Church in this dispensation.

May I leave you with my witness of this fact, that I know that he did, that day in the grove, see God the Father and the Son, and that he was their instrument in the establishment of this work. I leave you with this testimony in the name of Jesus Christ. Amen.

Joseph Smith's Christlike Attributes

Jack H Goaslind

In late May the Mississippi River runs swift and high, sparkling and bubbling in the midday sunlight. Birds sing; the air is redolent with fragrances; distantly you can hear a soft Sabbath bell toll; the earth and all about is richly abundant with life.

Some eleven miles to the east, across the farmlands away from the great Mississippi, stands the small town of Carthage, Illinois. On Sunday, May 21, of this year, my family and I solemnly walked the paths of Carthage and examined anew the momentous events of that place.

I could not help but look toward today's assignment, knowing I would stand before you marvelous and gifted students at BYU and your devoted administration and faculty, wanting and wishing with all my heart that each of you could feel what I was feeling at that moment as I tried to absorb it and take it all in—knowing this would be the exact anniversary of the Martyrdom of the Prophet Joseph Smith and of his brother Hyrum Smith, June 27, 1995. One hundred and fifty-one years ago today, Joseph, the prophet of the Restoration,

Jack H Goaslind was a member of the First Quorum of the Seventy of The Church of Jesus Christ of Latter-day Saints when this devotional address was given at Brigham Young University on 27 June 1995. © *Intellectual Reserve, Inc.*

and Hyrum, patriarch of the Church, gave their individual lives for the sake of their testimony of Jesus Christ.

In the fifth hour after noon, each suffered multiple shots. It is interesting, and I think even important, that in Jewish symbolism the number *five* denotes sanctification and/or purification. Five hours after noonday Joseph and Hyrum died.

Neither brother sought death, but it was not unforeseen. Joseph had forebodings as early as April 1829, when the Lord told him, "And even if they do unto you even as they have done unto me, blessed are ye, for you shall dwell with me in glory" (D&C 6:30). Joseph went to Carthage, in his words, "like a lamb to the slaughter" (D&C 135:4). The ruthless death of these brothers was their final witness of the Savior whom they served. As John Taylor wrote of Joseph:

Like most of the Lord's anointed in ancient times, [he] *has sealed his mission and his works with his own blood. . . .*

. . . The testators are now dead, and their testament is in force. [D&C 135:3, 5]

In sealing his testimony with his blood, Joseph followed the pattern of the Savior. It was in reference to the Savior, the "mediator of the new testament," that Paul taught, "For where a testament is, there must also of necessity be the death of the testator. For a testament is of force after men are dead" (Hebrews 9:15–17). I will never forget Carthage and the impression it left on my soul. Nauvoo was next. This is where I met a missionary couple whose strong and humble witness of Joseph so affected me that I asked if they would write down their feelings for me about their mission in the City of Joseph. A few weeks ago I received a reply from Elder and Sister Wood that seems appropriate here. They said:

Since our call to serve a mission at the Nauvoo Visitors' Center, our knowledge and testimony of the Prophet Joseph Smith has grown immensely. We [already] *knew that Joseph Smith was a prophet of God. . . . We also knew that he had undergone many trials for the Church, but we didn't*

know or realize just what he endured and to what lengths and depths he
went to help bring forth the kingdom of God and restore it to the earth.

One day, while testifying to a couple in front of the Christus [statue]
that Jesus Christ gave his life and atoned for our sins so we, his brothers and
sisters, might return to live with our Heavenly Father, I suddenly realized
more fully that Joseph Smith gave [up] *his life, too, . . . that we might have*
the fullness of the gospel.

Both the Savior and the Prophet Joseph gave their lives in a
divine cause. Yet President David O. McKay once wrote, "I confess
that [Christ's shedding His blood] has moved me less than the realiza-
tion that in His life He lived for His fellow men" ("The Atonement,"
Instructor, March 1959, p. 66). Similarly, I am more inspired by
Joseph Smith's life than by his death. Quoting John Taylor again, he
"left a fame and name that cannot be slain. He lived great" (D&C
135:3). It is vital to commemorate the Prophet's death; we must never
forget. Yet his life is a model of one possessed of mighty faith in
Jesus Christ. The Lord asked the Nephites, "What manner of men
ought ye to be?" and then answered his own question, "Even as I am"
(see 3 Nephi 27:27). The Lord is our model and guide or, in Joseph
Smith's words, "the prototype or standard of salvation" (*Lectures on
Faith,* comp. N. B. Lundwall [Salt Lake City: Bookcraft, 1959 (1972
printing)], p. 63). To be saved is to become like our Savior. We
measure our spiritual progress against this standard. Joseph Smith
so faithfully emulated the Master that he too becomes a model, a
standard by which we can gauge our spirituality.

Because Joseph patterned his life after the Savior, whom he
knew so well, we can better follow the Savior's pattern. Joseph Smith
taught:

When men begin to live by faith they begin to draw near to God; and when
faith is perfected they are like him; and because he is saved they are saved
also; for they will be in the same situation he is in, because they have come to
him; and when he appears they shall be like him, for they will see him as he
is. [*Lectures on Faith,* pp. 62–63]

Nephi wrote, "Unless a man shall endure to the end, in following the example of the Son of the living God, he cannot be saved" (2 Nephi 31:16). By looking at some of the Savior's divine attributes, we can compare them with Joseph Smith's life to see how he patterned it after his Lord. This can be a powerful reminder of what we must do to be saved or to become like Jesus Christ.

The beloved disciple John stated simply, "God is love" (1 John 4:16). Kindness and compassion flowed from the Only Begotten Son's soul as pure water from a pristine spring. Sacrifice and service were as natural to him as eating and sleeping are to us.

One of my favorite examples of the Lord's love is his raising of Lazarus, the brother of Mary and Martha. Lazarus was sick, and his sisters sent for the Lord, saying, "He whom thou lovest is sick." We are also told that "Jesus loved Martha, and her sister, and Lazarus." Jesus had perfect faith that he could restore Lazarus to health, as he had done on numerous occasions with others. In this instance he had both temporal and spiritual purposes in mind. He had tarried two days, and Lazarus had died. He said, "I am glad for your sakes that I was not there, to the intent ye may believe; nevertheless let us go unto him." When Jesus arrived in Judea, Lazarus had lain in the grave for four days. His sisters were sorrowful. Martha said, "If thou hadst been here, my brother had not died." Even so, Martha was trusting, and said, "But I know, that even now, whatsoever thou wilt ask of God, God will give it thee." Jesus taught Martha, "I am the resurrection, and the life: he that believeth in me, though he were dead, yet shall he live." When Jesus arrived at the grave, he saw the two sisters and others weeping. Jesus "groaned in the spirit, and was troubled." Then "Jesus wept." Jesus mourned for his friend Lazarus. The law of mourning instructs: "Thou shalt live together in love, insomuch that thou shalt weep for the loss of them that die" (D&C 42:45). The Lord deeply felt Mary's and Martha's anguish along with his own. Lazarus was restored to his family, and many believed on Jesus (see John 11:1–46). This gives us hope that we can indeed, one day, be like him, for we have glimpsed him as he is.

Joseph Smith taught this principle of love:

Love is one of the chief characteristics of Deity, and ought to be manifested by those who aspire to be the sons of God. A man filled with the love of God, is not content with blessing his family alone, but ranges through the whole world, anxious to bless the whole human race. [*Teachings*, p. 174]

He further said, "I love your soul, and the souls of the children of men, and pray and do all I can for the salvation of all" (*Teachings*, p. 22). Among those who knew Joseph's charity and regard was a nineteen-year-old young man named William Taylor, who spent two weeks with the Prophet. William said, "I have never known the same joy and satisfaction in the companionship of any other person" (*Young Woman's Journal* 17 [1906], p. 548). It was remarked of Joseph that "he did not like to pass a child, however small, without speaking to it" (Lyman O. Littlefield, "The Prophet Joseph Smith in Zion's Camp," *Juvenile Instructor* 27, no. 4 [15 February 1892]: 109). There are stories of Joseph picking flowers for children or drying their tears or wiping mud from their shoes. Thus, Joseph humbly followed his Savior's lead in loving and blessing little children.

At the funeral of Lorenzo Barnes, he exclaimed, "O that I had the language of the archangel to express my feelings once to my friends! But I never expect to in this life" (*Teachings*, p. 296). As mayor of Nauvoo, Joseph was called upon to render judgment on Anthony, a black man who had not only been selling liquor in violation of the law but had been doing it on the Sabbath. Anthony implored Joseph for leniency, stating that he needed money to buy the freedom of his child held as a slave in a southern state. Joseph said, "I am sorry, Anthony, but the law must be observed, and we will have to impose a fine." The next day Joseph gave Anthony a fine horse to purchase the freedom of the child. Joseph's largeness of soul is legendary. He wrote, "It is a duty which every Saint ought to render to his brethren freely—to always love them, and ever succor them. To be justified before God we must love one another" (*Teachings*, p. 76). To show love in this same spirit is a decision each of you can make today, even at this moment.

President Spencer W. Kimball, another great prophetic example of love, taught:

> *One can learn to be loving. If one patterns his life in the mold of love—if he consciously and determinedly directs his thoughts, controls his acts, and tries to feel and constantly express his love, he becomes a person of love, for "As he thinketh in his heart, so is he." (Proverbs 23:7.)* [*TSWK,* pp. 245–46]

You could at this moment think of someone, picture a face or think of a name, and then connect it with some act of service you could perform. If you will try this, with real intent, you will be inspired. You will know what to do. Of course, then, after you know, you must do. Act on the inspiration you receive. You will become a loving person after the pattern of Jesus and Joseph.

Love, then, is an attribute developed by choice, a deliberate decision to follow the Lord. I remind you, however, that even Jesus experienced obstacles to love, just as we do. For example, he suffered "hunger, thirst, and fatigue, even more than man can suffer" (Mosiah 3:7), but he served anyway. All of the kind, compassionate, loving things that Christ did were done in the shadow of the cross.

Consider, for example, his conversation with the Samaritan woman at the well. Jesus and his disciples were journeying from Judea to Galilee. The record states that he stopped at Jacob's well, "being wearied with his journey," and his disciples went to buy meat. Despite his weariness, he took time to teach the woman of Samaria. The record does not state whether he was ever able to rest. Apparently he did not, because the Samaritans "besought him that he would tarry with them: and he abode there two days. And many more believed because of his own word" (see John 4:1–42). We can be grateful that he sacrificed rest for responsibility. His words about living water have refreshed and brought rest to multitudes throughout the centuries.

In a comparable way, all that Joseph Smith did was in the shadow of Carthage. Persecution of the darkest hue began the first time he recounted his experience of the First Vision.

Four months after the Church was organized, he was told, "Be patient in afflictions, for thou shalt have many" (D&C 24:8). On the one hand, picture Joseph Smith ministering to the Saints, directing the affairs of an infant church, sending missionaries abroad, building temples, and leading his family. On the other hand, picture Joseph hiding from false accusers; dealing with contrived legal charges; enduring unjust imprisonment; hearing news of the murder, rape, and torture of his beloved Saints; coping with the venom of apostates; suffering beatings, attempted poisonings, and other mob lunacy.

He once wrote, "My family was kept in a continual state of alarm, not knowing, when I went from home, that I should ever return again; or what would befall me from day to day" (*Times and Seasons* 1, p. 3). His burdens were beyond our comprehension. To paraphrase Isaiah, it is a vexation of the spirit just to hear the report of his troubles (see Isaiah 28:19).

The Prophet was not adverse to introspection, even when prompted by scurrilous tales. Stories about Joseph, many of them twisted or blatantly false, circulated constantly. Yet the Prophet said something like this:

> *When I have heard of a story about me, I sit down and think about it and pray about it, and I ask myself the question, "Did I say something or was there something about my manner to give some basis for that story to start?" And often if I think about it long enough, I realize I have done something to give that basis. And there wells up in me a forgiveness of the person who has told that story, and a resolve that I will never do that thing again.* [See *They Knew the Prophet*, comp. Hyrum L. Andrus and Helen Mae Andrus (Salt Lake City: Bookcraft, 1974), p. 144]

Joseph's soul was enlarged through suffering. Too many in our day, even among Church members, become contracted through trials or ill fate. Rather than forgetting themselves in service, they

withdraw into shells of bitterness and self-pity. All of us have trials
and temptations adapted to our capacity. After all, this is mortality. It
does no good to ask, "Why me?" Rather, we should concede, "Why
not me?" and become more like him.

President Kimball also gave profound counsel in this area:

> *Only when you lift a burden, God will lift your burden. Divine paradox
> this! The man who staggers and falls because his burden is too great can
> lighten that burden by taking on the weight of another's burden. You get by
> giving, but your part of giving must be given first.* [*TSWK*, p. 251]

Both the Lord and the Prophet Joseph gave and gave and gave.
Both were ministers of salvation. Their service and sacrifice extended
to all mankind in love.

To Moses, the Lord said, "For behold, this is my work and my
glory—to bring to pass the immortality and eternal life of man"
(Moses 1:39). The Savior's mission was centered on others' spiritual
and temporal welfare. President J. Reuben Clark, Jr., said that the
Savior left as a heritage for his Church the carrying on of two great
activities:

> *Work for the relief of the ills and the sufferings of humanity, and the
> teaching of the spiritual truths which should bring us back into the presence
> of our Heavenly Father.* [*CR*, April 1937, p.22]

Thus we see the Savior healing the lepers, giving sight to the
blind, causing the infirm to leap to their feet, and bringing comfort to
all who would believe. He set a precedent of service. He went about
relieving the ills and sufferings to which mortals are natural heirs.

In addition, the Savior taught gospel principles. His Sermon
on the Mount, repeated and amplified among the Nephites, is
unparalleled. His teachings concerning the bread of life and the living
water are transcendent truths. When some of his disciples murmured
because of his teachings, the Savior said, "The words that I speak
unto you, they are spirit, and they are life" (John 6:63). The Lord

invited all to believe in him and to be born again, and in Mosiah's words, to be "changed from their carnal and fallen state, to a state of righteousness, being redeemed of God, becoming his sons and daughters" (Mosiah 27:25). Joseph emulated the Savior's devotion to the salvation of all mankind. As president of the Church, he organized the united order to bless the Saints temporally. He taught:

We must visit the fatherless and the widow in their affliction, and we must keep ourselves unspotted from the world: for such virtues flow from the great fountain of pure religion, strengthening our faith by adding every good quality that adorns the children of the blessed Jesus, we can pray in the season of prayer; we can love our neighbor as ourselves, and be faithful in tribulation, knowing that the reward of such is greater in the kingdom of heaven. What a consolation! What a joy! Let me live the life of the righteous, and let my reward be like his! [Teachings, p. 76]

Joseph ministered in power to relieve the considerable suffering experienced by the Saints. On what was referred to as the "day of God's power," July 22, 1839, the Prophet lay stricken with a vile disease, as were many of the Saints. Neighbor cared for neighbor, parents for children, and children for parents. There were so many ill that the caregivers were overwhelmed and exhausted. Moved upon by the Spirit, Joseph rose from his sickbed and went across the river to Montrose, Iowa. Dozens were immediately healed on that day. He states in his journal, "Many of the sick were this day raised by the power of God" (in B. H. Roberts, *New Witnesses for God: I. Joseph Smith, the Prophet* [Salt Lake City: Deseret News, 1911], p. 259). The Prophet Joseph also followed the Savior in teaching the gospel of salvation. Through modern revelation, comforting and exalting doctrines were revealed to him. The Lord told him, "This generation shall have my word through you" (D&C 5:10). In 1841 the Prophet "told the brethren that the Book of Mormon was the most correct of any book on earth, and the keystone of our religion, and a man would get nearer to God by abiding by its precepts, than by any other book" (*HC* 4:461). Plain and precious truths were restored through Joseph

Smith's inspired translation of sacred records, bringing generations to an understanding of their Lord and Savior. We measure our fidelity to God's word through the principles revealed in the Book of Mormon.

Who besides Joseph has offered the world such a saving book? Who can match him? Who in this dispensation has surpassed the King Follett Discourse, for example? Where can we find a greater statement on faith than the *Lectures on Faith*, which were prepared under his tutelage? Who has mastered the ordinances and principles of temple worship better than he through whom the keys were restored? Joseph Smith was, indeed, a teacher of supernal truths. Brigham Young said of him:

The excellency of the glory of the character of brother Joseph Smith was that he could reduce heavenly things to the understanding of the finite. When he preached to the people . . . he reduced his teachings to the capacity of every man, woman, and child, making them as plain as a well-defined pathway. [*JD* 8:206]

Therefore, our duty is to minister to the needs and wants of others, both temporally and spiritually. Joseph Smith taught, "Let the Saints remember that great things depend on their individual exertion, and that they are called to be co-workers with us and the Holy Spirit in accomplishing the great work of the last days" (*Teachings*, p. 178). In the last general conference President Gordon B. Hinckley taught our responsibility:

We are all in this great endeavor together. . . . Your obligation is as serious in your sphere of responsibility as is my obligation in my sphere. No calling in this church is small or of little consequence. All of us in the pursuit of our duty touch the lives of others. To each of us in our respective responsibilities the Lord has said: "Wherefore, be faithful; stand in the office which I have appointed unto you; succor the weak, lift up the hands which hang down, and strengthen the feeble knees" (D&C 81:5). ["This Is the Work of the Master," *Ensign*, May 1995, p. 71]

Your life, as President Stephen L. Richards used to say, is a mission, not a career. If you are wise, you will prepare for a life of service.

One reason for the Prophet's serenity in distress was his total, unflinching commitment to God's will. A dictionary definition of faith is "belief and trust in and loyalty to God." Joseph Smith loved God with a fervor born of personal experience, for he had seen him. He knew his power and glory. His trust was complete. His loyalty was unquestioning.

Jesus was the greatest person ever to walk this earth. He had infinitely greater wisdom and power than any man. He had power over life and death. He could command the elements. Yet he said, "I can of mine own self do nothing: . . . because I seek not mine own will, but the will of the Father which hath sent me" (John 5:30). President Joseph F. Smith saw in vision "the hosts of the dead . . . who had offered sacrifice in the similitude of the great sacrifice of the Son of God" (D&C 138:11–13). How can our sacrifices be in the similitude of the Savior's great infinite and eternal sacrifice? We can submit our wills to the Father's. Rather than persisting in our own "carnal wills and desires," our will, like the "will of the Son," should be "swallowed up in the will of the Father" (see Mosiah 16:12 and 15:7). This is how Christ lived, and this is how Joseph Smith lived. Such submission to God led ultimately to death. Joseph's martyrdom was indeed in similitude of the Lord's great sacrifice, for he went where he was sent and did what he did knowing full well where it would lead.

Brigham Young said, "I heard Joseph say many a time, 'I shall not live until I am forty years of age'" (*DBY,* p. 467). Yet Joseph also stated confidently, "God will always protect me until my mission is fulfilled" (*Teachings,* p. 366). The chances that you and I will be called upon to die for our convictions is remote. How then can we offer a sacrifice in similitude of the great sacrifice of the Son of God? President Marion G. Romney said:

I decided in my youth that for me the best approach to the solution of problems and the resolving of questions would be to proceed as Jesus proceeded: foster an earnest desire to do the Lord's will; familiarize myself with what the Lord has revealed on the matters involved; pray with diligence and faith for an inspired understanding of his will and the courage to do it. ["What Would Jesus Do?" *New Era*, September 1972, p. 5]

The Savior concluded his mortal life as he began it—in purity and innocence. Judas painfully recognized that he had "betrayed the innocent blood" (Matthew 27:4), and Pilate called the Lord a "just person" (Matthew 27:24). Jesus was a lamb without spot or blemish. He was the sinless Son of God. His death insured that salvation could come to all who believe and obey.

Joseph Smith also concluded his life as it began—humble and obedient. He had fulfilled his mission. He said, "I have a conscience void of offense towards God, and towards all men. I shall die innocent" (D&C 135:4). Elder Neal A. Maxwell said:

The Prophet Joseph Smith, of course, was not a perfect man. There has been only one such—Jesus Christ. But Joseph Smith was a special witness for Jesus Christ. . . . We do not, as some occasionally charge, worship Joseph Smith, nor place him on a par with Jesus. But we do venerate him, remembering, hopefully, that the highest and best form of veneration is emulation. ["The Prophet Joseph Smith: Spiritual Statesman," Annual Joseph Smith Memorial Sermons, Logan, Utah, 19 January 1975, p. 12]

My friends in Nauvoo, Elder and Sister Woods, have a deep and abiding love for the Savior and his servant Joseph Smith. They said, "Every day our experiences here give more indications of [their] greatness." To close their letter, the Woods spoke about the spirit of Joseph that still permeates the City Beautiful and related a tender experience about John.

John (not his real name), about thirty years old, walked into the visitors' center alone, where he was greeted by the Woods and asked if he'd like to take a tour—the Woods asked how much time he had.

John answered, "As long as it takes to see it all." John said he was a member but had not been inside a church in almost twenty years.

I paraphrase Brother Woods' story as follows:

I was prompted to conduct him as though he knew nothing about the Church and began the tour about the founding of Nauvoo, the First Vision, the coming forth of the Book of Mormon, and the organization of the Church. I asked him often, "Do you remember hearing about that in Primary?" And many times he affirmed that he did remember.

I bore my testimony to John. Next I took him into the theater to see Remembering Nauvoo. *John was the only one there for the film. As the movie began, I withdrew, but returned twenty minutes later just as John exited. He had enjoyed the presentation, and we continued the tour.*

This part includes details about the city of Nauvoo and its temple— during which we arrived at the Christus *statue, where we played the message of the Savior. Generally I don't bear my testimony here, but for some reason I sat down beside him and afterward bore my testimony about Jesus Christ.*

I saw tears come to his eyes and felt impressed to say, "John, when you return home to Florida, will you seek out your bishop and tell him you want to become actively involved in the Church? Ask him what you have to do, and he will advise and help you all the way." John looked me in the eye and promised me he would do that. The tour continued to the martyrdom scene, and I again bore testimony—this time as to Joseph Smith being a true prophet. Again John's eyes moistened [and] we continued on to the Saints' arrival in Salt Lake and the temple there. I explained that my temple marriage to Sister Wood was for time and eternity—if we live worthy. John said, "Awesome."

We completed the tour and said our emotional good-byes. But John stopped and turned and said, "Can I ask you a very important question?" I answered, "By all means." John asked, "When you started the movie, did you stay in the theater with me or did you leave?" I told him I had left— why? John answered with tears in his eyes, "All during the movie I kept looking over my shoulder to see who else was in the theater." I asked him who he thought was there. He said, "I guess my grandparents are trying to tell me to clean up my act." By this point he was crying openly. We embraced and wept joyful tears together. I told him I loved him and knew he was sent to us not by chance. Elder Wood closed this account by saying, "It is the spirit . . . of Joseph Smith [in Nauvoo] that allows experiences like this . . . and gives us the hope and courage to carry on and endure to the end."

In closing, I testify to these words in section 135 of the Doctrine and Covenants: "Joseph Smith, the Prophet and Seer of the Lord, has done more, save Jesus only, for the salvation of men in this world, than any other man that ever lived in it" (D&C 135:3). And I say, "Praise to the man who communed with Jehovah! Jesus anointed that Prophet and Seer" ("Praise to the Man," *Hymns*, 1985, no. 27). Joseph knew Jesus! He communed with him in our behalf. He was a chosen vessel of the Lord to whom angels ministered, thus preparing "the way that the residue of men may have faith in Christ, that the Holy Ghost may have place in their hearts" (Moroni 7:32).

May we, too, come to know the Lord, commune with him, and learn to be like him, as did Brother Joseph, I pray in the name of Jesus Christ. Amen.

Joseph Smith: The Prophet

David B. Haight

As I look out into the faces of you precious young sons and daughters of our Heavenly Father and sense your unlimited potential to "do good unto all men" (Galatians 6:10), I pray tonight that each of you—and that I—will be blessed with the Spirit of the Lord, that what I testify of will strengthen your faith and desire to personally live and be faithful to all the true principles of God's eternal plan of salvation—those keys and powers that have been conferred upon all men during these latter days, a fulfillment of the declaration of Paul to the Ephesians "that in the dispensation of the fulness of times he might gather together in one all things in Christ, both which are in heaven, and which are on earth; even in him" (Ephesians 1:10).

THE RESTORATION

The principles, doctrines, and ordinances of the gospel of our Lord Jesus Christ have been revealed anew, including a knowledge of the true nature of God—a personal, loving, Eternal Father—and of

David B. Haight was a member of the Quorum of the Twelve Apostles of The Church of Jesus Christ of Latter-day Saints when this fireside address was given at Brigham Young University on 2 March 1986. © Intellectual Reserve, Inc.

Jesus Christ, the literal Son of God, of whose divinity there has come another witness in the Book of Mormon. The words of Ezekiel that the stick of Judah (the Bible) shall be joined with the stick of Joseph (the Book of Mormon) as a testimony of two nations have found their fulfillment (see Ezekiel 37:15–22). This I solemnly declare to all of you.

The authority to act in the name of God, the holy priesthood, has been conferred upon men in our time by those same individuals who held it anciently—Peter, James, and John—apostles of our Lord who were ordained by the Savior himself when he was upon the earth.

The Church of Jesus Christ has been reestablished. The priesthood of God is again among men. God has revealed himself anew for the blessing of his children.

As I declare to you, my dear young friends, these divine events— with all the characteristics of the Church of the early apostles, including the personal direction of Jesus Christ, divinely revealed doctrine, divinely chosen leaders, continuous revelation, and the witness of the Holy Ghost to all who obey—I testify that the instrument through whom this divine revelation came was one foreordained—the youthful Joseph Smith—whose faith and desire brought about "one of the most significant religious events in the history of mankind" (Milton V. Backman, Jr., "Joseph Smith's Recitals of the First Vision," *Ensign*, Jan. 1985, p. 8).

Since my early youth I have believed and carried in my mind a vivid picture of the teen-age Joseph finding a secluded spot, kneeling in the quiet grove, and in childlike faith asking the desire of his heart. He must have felt assured the Lord would hear and somehow answer him. There appeared to him two glorious personages, a description of whom, he said, was beyond his ability to express.

I have been blessed, as the years have passed, with unusual experiences with people, places, and personal events of an intimate, spiritual nature, and, through the power of the Holy Ghost, I have received an ever-deepening witness and knowledge of this heaven-directed restoration of the Lord's plan of salvation. The events related by Joseph Smith of the Restoration are true.

THE VISION

Each of you can develop in your bosom an uplifting, sanctifying, and glorifying feeling of its truth. The Holy Ghost will reveal and seal upon each of your hearts this knowledge, if you truly desire. Our understanding, belief, and faith in "the vision" (as we refer to it) of God the Father and his Only Begotten Son appearing to Joseph, thereby ushering in this final dispensation with its great and precious truths, is essential to our eternal salvation. Salvation comes only through Christ. Joseph Smith is the instrument or revealer of that knowledge, divinely called to teach of the terms and conditions of the Father's plan and given the keys of salvation for all mankind.

The knowledge is mine that God did reveal himself unto Joseph—his witness of this final dispensation. We now know something of the form, features, and even character of that mighty intelligence whose wisdom, creation, and power control the affairs of the universe. God made it known that Jesus Christ is the express image of the Father.

In Joseph's own words, the brightness was above anything he had ever known. He looked up. Before him stood two glorious personages. One of them, pointing to the other, said, "This is My Beloved Son. Hear Him!" (JS—H 1:17).

It might have seemed inconceivable to young Joseph that he was looking upon God our Heavenly Father and his Son—that the Lord had come to visit and instruct him.

The Son, bidden by the Father, spoke to the kneeling boy. Joseph was told that all the churches were wrong. They had corrupted the doctrine; they had broken the ordinances and had lost the authority of the priesthood of God. He was told that the leaders of the man-made churches were displeasing to the Lord, that they were collecting money which should be given freely, and that the time for the restoration of all truth and authority had come, including the organization of the Church. Then, to his infinite astonishment, he was told that *he*, Joseph Smith—young, unlearned, but humble—was to be the instrument through whom the Almighty would reestablish his work in these, the latter days—the gospel never to be taken away again.

Such was the glorious beginning of the restoration of the Church of Jesus Christ.

Some three years later, as he was beginning to mature, Joseph Smith had another heavenly visitation. This time an angel sent from the presence of God informed Joseph that he was Moroni and revealed to the young man the resting place of a set of gold plates upon which certain ancient inhabitants of America had recorded the history of their peoples. In the course of time, these records were translated by the gift and power of God and published early in 1830.

A DEFINITE PURPOSE

The Book of Mormon is the most remarkable book in the world from a doctrinal, historical, or philosophical point of view. Its integrity has been assailed with senseless fury for over a century and a half; yet its position and influence today is more impregnable than ever. The Book of Mormon did not come forth as a curiosity. It was written with a definite purpose—a purpose to be felt by every reader. From the title page we read that it was written "to the convincing of the Jew and Gentile that Jesus is the Christ, the Eternal God, manifesting himself unto all nations." The message it contains is a witness for Christ and teaches the love of God for all mankind. Its purpose is to bring people to accept Jesus as the Christ. The book tells of the actual visit of Christ to ancient America and records the teachings and instructions he gave in clarity and great power to the people. The Book of Mormon substantiates the Bible in its teachings of the Savior, speaks of Christ more than any other subject, and teaches that our Savior is the Redeemer and Atoner of mankind, constantly emphasizing that he is the central figure in God's plan of salvation. This divine record makes converts to its message and to his Church, which teaches it.

I have marveled at God's wisdom in bringing forth this ancient record in the manner in which it was accomplished, for it has also become the powerful witness of the divine mission of Joseph Smith. Sunday, November 28, 1841, the Prophet wrote:

I spent the day in the council with the Twelve Apostles at the house of President Young, conversing with them upon a variety of subjects. Brother Joseph Fielding was present, having been absent four years on a mission to England. I told the brethren that the Book of Mormon was the most correct of any book on earth, and the keystone of our religion, and a man would get nearer to God by abiding by its precepts, than by any other book. [HC 4:461]

Joseph Smith was foreordained to be the duly appointed leader of this, the greatest and final of all dispensations. After the angel Moroni's visit, other heavenly messengers conferred upon Joseph holy priesthood authority, divine keys, power, and revelations from God.

Not only was the Church organized under inspiration and divine direction, but the necessary body of doctrine for guidance of the Church was revealed. Faith and light were again available to distill the darkness that was upon the earth. Joseph Smith, after seeking and being taught by the Author of Truth, learned that

1. God is in form like man.

2. He has a voice; he speaks.

3. He is considerate and kind.

4. He answers prayers.

5. His son is obedient to the Father and is the mediator between God and man.

6. "The Father has a body of flesh and bones as tangible as man's; the Son also; but the Holy Ghost has not a body of flesh and bones, but is a personage of Spirit" (D&C 130:22).

Though Hebrew scriptures make references to temples and baptism for the deceased, Joseph Smith was the first to have revealed the purpose of temples and salvation for all—including those who have passed on without having received a knowledge of the gospel—along with the eternal marriage covenant and sealing of man and woman as the foundation for exaltation.

Joseph Smith, speaking at the first conference of the Church in June 1830, spoke of great happiness "to find ourselves engaged in the

very same order of things as observed by the holy Apostles of old"
(*HC* 1:85).

A PROPHET OF THE LORD

Under the inspiration of Almighty God, the Church began to
flourish. The Lord's promise that a "marvelous work is about to come
forth" was being fulfilled in a miraculous way (see D&C 4:1). The
gospel message spread rapidly. The missionary spirit was touching
hearts. The Book of Mormon was being read. Tens, then hundreds,
then thousands joined the Church. The Lord, speaking through
Joseph, proclaimed:

*For verily the voice of the Lord is unto all men, and there is none to
escape; and there is no eye that shall not see, neither ear that shall not hear,
neither*

heart that shall not be penetrated. . . .

*The weak things of the world shall come forth and break down the
mighty and strong ones, that man should not counsel his fellow man, neither
trust in the arm of flesh—*

*But that every man might speak in the name of God the Lord, even the
Savior of the world; . . .*

*That the fulness of my gospel might be proclaimed. . . unto the ends of
the world, and before kings and rulers.* [D&C 1:2, 19–20, 23]

Politicians began worrying over this new phenomenon. Enemies
were organizing, and the Prophet's life was becoming endangered.
After months of imprisonment in the dark, damp dungeon known as
Liberty Jail, a discouraged Joseph cried out to the Lord:

*O God, where art thou? And where is the pavilion that covereth thy
hiding place?*

*How long shall thy hand be stayed, and thine eye, . . . behold from the
eternal heavens the wrongs of thy people and of thy servants, . . .*

Yea, O Lord, how long shall they suffer these wrongs and unlawful oppressions, before thine heart shall be softened toward them. [D&C 121:1–3]

Then a loving, answering Savior promised Joseph:

The ends of the earth shall inquire after thy name, and fools shall have thee in derision, and hell shall rage against thee;

While the pure in heart, and the wise, and the noble, and the virtuous, shall seek counsel, and authority, and blessings constantly from under thy hand.

And thy people shall never be turned against thee by the testimony of traitors.

. . . Thou shalt be had in honor; . . . and thy voice shall be more terrible in the midst of thine enemies than the fierce lion, because of thy righteousness; and thy God shall stand by thee forever and ever. [D&C 122:1–4]

In his last public address to a large congregation in Nauvoo, Joseph said:

I do not regard my own life. I am ready to be offered a sacrifice for this people; for what can our enemies do? Only kill the body, and their power is then at an end. Stand firm, my friends; never flinch. Do not seek to save your lives, for he that is afraid to die for the truth will lose eternal life. . . .

God has tried you. You are a good people; therefore I love you with all my heart. Greater love hath no man than that he should lay down his life for his friends. You have stood by me in the hour of trouble, and I am willing to sacrifice my life for your preservation. [George Q. Cannon, *Life of Joseph Smith the Prophet* (Salt Lake City: Deseret Book Co., 1907), p. 498]

This statement is all the more remarkable as the Prophet was still in the morning of life—only thirty-eight years old—and great as he had already become, the zenith of his mental and spiritual powers had not yet been reached. Life was precious to him with all its possibilities of future achievements. Yet he was willing to give it up, willing to forego all the honors that might be his, the greatness that would come to him if he lived.

"A Prophet," wrote Truman Madsen, "is one who, in fulfillment of his mission, undergoes great suffering, yet through it all, is radiant. A Prophet, in short, is a saint."

Someone has written:

> *Nowhere in the long lists of martyrs, save only in the case of Joseph Smith, do we find one who voluntarily went out of his way to die for his faith and people. In that fateful hour when the choice of life or death was to be made, Joseph Smith did not hedge, or sidestep, or seek to save his life, but bravely chose to die, in the hope that his people might henceforth be free to worship God in their own way, and that the testimony which he had borne of a restored gospel might be sanctified [if necessary] by the shedding of his blood.*

"Had he been spared a martyr's fate till mature manhood," said Parley P. Pratt, "he was certainly endowed with power and ability to have [influenced] the world in many respects."

One may pick up the thread of Joseph Smith's life on any day of any year and find incalculable suffering, both his own and the disciples' around him.

"BE PATIENT IN AFFLICTIONS"

Mormonism was appearing to become, as the scripture says, as a stone cut out of a mountain, without hands and rolling forth to fill the whole earth (see D&C 65:2). Political officials worried about it moving outward and abroad from the immediate locale, illegal charges were leveled, court documents and summons were issued, and vigilantes were formed—at Carthage, the county seat. Joseph and Hyrum were to appear to answer charges against them.

As Joseph Smith left Nauvoo for Carthage that twenty-fourth day of June, he would have looked for the last time on the city and the magnificent temple that he loved. He knew he would never look upon it again.

"Be patient in afflictions," he was told, "for thou shalt have many." Later, he said adversity had become second nature, but had only "wafted me that much closer to Deity." Brigham Young said of him that he lived one thousand years in thirty-eight.

To his companions who were accompanying him to Carthage, he gave these prophetic words:

> *I am going like a lamb to the slaughter, but I am calm as a summer's morning; I have a conscience void of offense towards God, and towards all men. . . . And it shall yet be said of me—he was murdered in cold blood.* [D&C 135:4]

Why did he not turn back? There was time to escape. He was not yet in the hands of his enemies. Friends were at his side who would die for him if necessary. Some suggested he flee across the Mississippi where he would be safe. But he continued to Carthage.

Joseph must have recalled some of the dangers through which he had passed—like the winter night when a mob broke into his home and with curses and profanity tore him from the bedside of his wife and sick children and dragged him over the frozen ground, kicking and beating him until he was unconscious. When consciousness returned, they stripped him of his clothing and covered his naked body from head to foot with a coat of tar and feathers, forcing open his mouth to fill it with the same substance, then left him on the frozen ground to die of cold and exposure.

Riding to Carthage he might have recalled the time in Missouri when he and some of his brethren had been betrayed into the hands of their enemies. The leader of the mob convened a court; Joseph and his associates were placed on trial for their lives. They were convicted and all sentenced to be shot the next morning at eight o'clock in the public square in Far West. At the appointed hour they were duly led forth to be murdered, but a dispute among the mob saved them.

Without even being permitted to bid farewell to their families, they were taken from place to place and exhibited to jeering crowds while the Saints were told they would never see their leaders again. But Joseph cheered his fellow prisoners by announcing that none of them would suffer death.

"Be of good cheer, brethren," he said, "the word of the Lord came to me last night that our lives should be given us, . . . not one of our lives shall be taken" (*HC* 3:200).

As Joseph contemplated those dreary months of imprisonment in Missouri, he must have recalled the night, when confined in a dungeon, he rebuked the guards. He and his brethren were trying to get a little sleep, but were kept awake by the awful blasphemies and obscene jests of their jailers, who were recounting the dreadful deeds of robbery and murder they had committed among the Mormons. These were no idle boasts, for these awful atrocities had actually been committed. Suddenly, Joseph rose to his feet and, in a voice that seemed to shake the very building, cried out:

Silence, ye fiends of the infernal pit! In the name of Jesus Christ I rebuke you, and command you to be still; I will not live another minute and hear such language. Cease such talk, or you or I die this instant! [*HC* 3:208]

The effect must have been electric in its suddenness. Some begged his pardon while others slunk into the dark corners of Liberty Jail to hide their shame.

The power of Jesus Christ, whose name he had invoked in his rebuke, was upon him. His hands and feet were in chains, but these the guards did not see. They saw only the righteous anger in his shining face, and felt the divine power in his voice as he rebuked them.

But if Joseph's voice was terrible as the roaring lion in his rebuke of the wicked, it was soothing as a mother's voice in comfort to the righteous. In that same name and by the same authority with which he silenced the blasphemies of the guards, he had blessed little children, baptized repentant sinners, conferred the Holy Ghost, healed the sick, and spoken words of comfort and consolation to thousands.

"ARE YOU AFRAID TO DIE?"

It was midnight when the wagon journey from Nauvoo ended. Joseph and his brethren entered Carthage, and his fate was sealed. His enemies had awaited their coming with great anxiety. The governor, who was present, persuaded the mob to disperse that night by promising them that they should have full satisfaction.

The next day, after a hearing, Joseph was released on bail, but re-arrested on a trumped-up charge of treason. Bail was refused and Joseph and Hyrum were placed in Carthage Jail.

The last night of Joseph's life on earth he bore a powerful testimony, to the guards and others who assembled at the door of the jail, of the divinity of the Book of Mormon, also declaring that the gospel had been restored and the kingdom of God established on the earth. It was for this reason that he was incarcerated in prison, not for violating any law of God or man.

It was late at night when they tried to get some rest. At first Joseph and Hyrum occupied the only bed in the jail room, but a gunshot during the night and a disturbance led Joseph's friends to insist that he take a place between two of them on the floor. They would protect him with their own bodies. Joseph asked Elder Markham to use his arm for a pillow while they conversed, then he turned to Elder Dan Jones, on the other side, and whispered, "Are you afraid to die?" And this staunch friend answered, "Has that time come, think you? Engaged in such a cause, I do not think death would have many terrors."

Joseph replied, "You will yet see Wales, and fulfill the mission appointed you before you die" (*HC* 6:601).

The next morning, the fateful twenty-seventh of June, 1844, three of the brethren left the prison and only four remained—Joseph and Hyrum and two of the apostles, both of whom during the day offered to die for him. The day was spent in writing letters to their wives, conversing on principles of the gospel, and singing. Between three and four o'clock in the afternoon the Prophet requested Elder John Taylor to sing the words of "A Poor Wayfaring Man of Grief."

This comforting song breathes in every line the very spirit and message of Christ. Only a person who loved his Savior and his fellowmen would have requested to hear these words at such a time.

When Elder Taylor had finished the song, the Prophet's eyes were wet with tears, and he said, "Sing that song again, will you, John?" (Claire Noall, *Intimate Disciple; a Portrait of Willard Richards, Apostle to Joseph Smith—Cousin of Brigham Young* [Salt Lake City: University of Utah Press, 1957], p. 440).

John "replied that he did not feel like singing. He was oppressed with a sense of coming disaster" (*Life of Joseph Smith*, p. 524).

"You'll feel better once you begin, and so will I," replied Joseph (*Intimate Disciple*, p. 440).

Hyrum also pleaded with him to repeat the song. And Elder Taylor did.

This time his voice was even sadder and more tender than at first, and when he concluded, all were hushed, but four hearts beat faster for they had carefully listened to the fateful words:

My friendship's utmost zeal to try,
He asked if I for him would die.
The flesh was weak; my blood ran chill,
But my free spirit cried, "I will!"
[*Hymns*, 1985, no. 29]

The other three heard Joseph murmur as an echo to the song, "I will!"

The love of Christ was in the song; the love of man was there in that room in the Carthage Jail.

While this spirit of love and service for men expressed in song and prayer filled the hearts of all within the jail, the mob was gathering. The final details you know.

ONLY LOVE BEGETS LOVE

When the news of the awful crime reached Nauvoo, the citizens were overcome with grief and horror. Probably such universal sorrow had not been known in an American city before. The warm summer sun left them cold and chill. Their prophet and their patriarch were dead. What else mattered?

When the wagon carrying the bodies was still a long way off, the entire population of Nauvoo went out to meet it. No greater tribute was ever paid to mortal man than was paid that day to Joseph and Hyrum Smith. Such universal love from those who knew them best could never have been won by selfish and designing men. Only love begets love. Once when Joseph had been asked how he had acquired so many followers and retained them, he replied, "It is because I possess the principle of love. All that I offer the world is a good heart and good hand."

Sariah Workman, an early immigrant, wrote: "I felt a divine influence whenever I was in his presence."

John Taylor, who was wounded at Carthage and later became prophet, said of him:

Joseph Smith, the Prophet and Seer of the Lord, has done more, save Jesus only, for the salvation of men in this world, than any other man that ever lived in it. In the short space of twenty years, he has brought forth the Book of Mormon, which he translated by the gift and power of God, and has been the means of publishing it on two continents; has sent the fulness of the everlasting gospel, which it contained, to the four quarters of the earth; has brought forth the revelations and commandments which compose this book of Doctrine and Covenants, and many other wise documents and instructions for the benefit of the children of men; gathered many thousands of the Latter-day Saints, founded a great city, and left a fame and name that cannot be slain. He lived great, and he died great in the eyes of God and his people; and like most of the Lord's anointed in ancient times, has sealed his mission and his works with his own blood. [D&C 135:3]

I leave each of you my love and testament that God, our Father, lives, that Jesus is the Christ, the Son of the Living God, crucified for the sins of the world "to cleanse it from all unrighteousness; that through him all might be saved" (D&C 76:41–42).

He is our Redeemer, our Lord, our King. His kingdom is again established on the earth. In the year 1820, God, our Eternal Father, and his son Jesus Christ appeared to Joseph Smith, who was foreordained to be the instrument of the Restoration, which is The Church of Jesus Christ of Latter-day Saints. This Church, by divine direction, is preparing the world for his second coming—for he will come again. This I humbly declare in his holy name. Amen.

"Praise to the Man"

_____

Gordon B. Hinckley

I would like to say first that it is a very genuine pleasure to be with you tonight. It is always an inspiration to come to these firesides. I do not know why we call them firesides. The word connotes a small group of friends sitting about the hearth where a warm fire burns, talking with one another in an informal way. Tonight you are numbered in the thousands, and we have neither hearth nor fire; but I hope we can speak together as friends, and in a rather informal manner. I seek the direction of the Holy Spirit, because I wish for nothing more than to say to you those things which will add to your faith as we are met together in a spirit of worship.

I am responsible for the singing of that first song by the congregation: "Praise to the Man." I would like to say a word or two about that great hymn from the pen of W. W. Phelps.

Many years ago when at the age of twelve I was ordained a deacon, my father, who was president of our stake, took me to my first stake priesthood meeting. In those days these meetings were held on a week night. I recall that we went to the Tenth Ward building in Salt Lake City. He walked up to the stand, and I sat on the back row, feeling a little alone and uncomfortable in that hall filled with strong

Gordon B. Hinckley was a member of the Quorum of the Twelve Apostles of The Church of Jesus Christ of Latter-day Saints when this fireside address was given at BYU on 4 November 1979. © _Intellectual Reserve, Inc._

men who had been ordained to the priesthood of God. The meeting was called to order, the opening song was announced, and—as was then the custom—we all stood to sing. There were perhaps as many as four hundred there, for it was a very large stake. Together these men lifted their strong voices, some with the accents of the European lands from which they had come as converts and all singing with a great spirit of conviction and testimony:

Praise to the man who communed with Jehovah!
Jesus anointed that Prophet and Seer,
Blessed to open the last dispensation,
Kings shall extol him, and nations revere.
["Praise to the Man," *Hymns*, no. 147]

They were singing of the Prophet Joseph Smith, and as they did so there came into my young heart a great surge of love for and belief in the mighty Prophet of this dispensation. In my childhood I had been taught much of him in meetings and classes in our ward as well as in our home; but my experience in that stake priesthood meeting was different. I knew then, by the power of the Holy Ghost, that Joseph Smith was indeed a prophet of God.

It is true that during the years which followed there were times when that testimony wavered somewhat, particularly in the seasons of my undergraduate university work—not at this university, but at another.

However, that conviction never left me entirely; and it has grown stronger through the years, partly because of the challenges of those days which compelled me to read and study and make certain for myself. I think that all of you go through similar experiences. President Lee once said that our testimonies need renewing every day. In harmony with that principle, I wish to say a few words tonight about Joseph Smith. Perhaps I shall not say anything that is new to you, but I hope and pray that the very repetition of matters with which you may be familiar will stir within you a renewal and strengthening of your testimony.

I am led to this subject by a letter, which I read only Friday, written by a New York evangelist who with diatribe and hate lashed out against the Prophet Joseph, calling him a wicked imposter, a fraud, a fake, and a deceiver and declaring that he was undertaking a national campaign to prove it. I do not know whether anything will come of his campaign; whatever happens, it will not be significant. It may topple a few of the weak, but it will only strengthen the strong. And long after this man and others of his kind have gone down to silence, the name of Joseph Smith will ring with honor and love in the hearts of an ever-growing band of Latter-day Saints in an ever-increasing number of nations of the earth.

Two weeks ago today I was in Nauvoo, the City of Joseph, with two of my brethren of the First Quorum of the Seventy and twelve mission presidents and their wives for a mission presidents' seminar. The touch of autumn was on the land—the leaves golden, a little haze in the air, the nights cool, the days warm. The tourist season was over, and the old city was quiet and beautiful. We held our first meeting in the restored Seventies Hall, where in the 1840s men prepared themselves, through study and through teaching one another the doctrine of the Kingdom, to go out to declare the message of the gospel to the world. This was the forerunner of the Missionary Training Center. As we met in that and other homes and halls in Nauvoo, it was as if the figures of the past were with us—Joseph and Hyrum, Brigham Young, Heber C. Kimball, John Taylor, Wilford Woodruff, the brothers Pratt—Orson and Parley—and a host of others.

This was indeed Joseph's city. He was the prophet who planned it, and his followers had built it. It became the largest and the most impressive in the state of Illinois. With sturdy brick homes, with halls for worship, instruction, and entertainment, and with the magnificent temple standing on the crest of the slope up from the river, this community on the Mississippi was put together as if its builders were to be there for a century or more.

Here, before that tragic day at Carthage, the Prophet was at the zenith of his career. Standing the other day where he once stood, I thought of the events that had brought him there, reviewing in my mind his inheritance. I thought of his forebears who generations before had left the British Isles and come to Boston; of their lives in the New World, through five generations on his father's side and four on his mother's; of their labors in clearing the lands of Massachusetts, New Hampshire, and Vermont to build farms and homes; of their distinguished service in the War of Independence; of the adversities and the failures they experienced in trying to wrest a living from the granite hills among which they lived. I thought of the little boy, born in Sharon in December of 1805, given his father's name. I reflected on that terrifying period of sickness when typhus fever struck the family and osteomyelitis, with great pain and debilitating infection, settled in Joseph's leg. That was while the family lived in Lebanon, New Hampshire; and how remarkable it was that only a few miles away, at the academy in Hanover, was Dr. Nathan Smith, perhaps then the only surgeon in the United States—if not in the world—who had developed a procedure by which that infected leg might be saved.

But it was not to be accomplished without terrible suffering. In fact, today it is difficult to conceive of how the little boy stood it as his father held him in his arms and his mother walked and prayed among the trees of the farm to escape his screams while the surgeon made the long incision and with forceps broke off the portions of infected bone without benefit of anesthesia of any kind. Perhaps remembrance of that intense suffering made a little more bearable for Joseph Smith the later tarring and feathering at Kirtland, the foul jail at Liberty, and the shots of the mob at Carthage.

In my looking back from Nauvoo the other day I thought of the forces that moved the Smith family from generations of life in New England to western New York, where they had to come if the fore-ordained purposes of God were to be accomplished. I thought of the loss of the family farm, of poor crops in that thin soil, of the great freeze of 1816 when a killing frost in July forced upon them the decision to look elsewhere; then of the move to Palmyra, of the purchase of a farm in Manchester, and of the revival preachers who stirred the people and so confused a boy that he determined to ask God for that wisdom so lacking in the contending revivalists.

That was the real beginning of it all, as you know—that spring day in the year 1820 when he knelt among the trees, opened his mouth in prayer, and beheld a glorious vision in which he spoke with God the Eternal Father and His Son, the risen Lord Jesus Christ. Then followed the years of instruction, the instructor an angel of God who on a dozen occasions taught, rebuked, warned, and comforted the boy as he grew into the young man.

And so, while in Nauvoo the other day I reflected on the preparation for prophethood: I reflected on this amazing Joseph Smith. I cannot expect his detractors, including the writer of the letter I read on Friday, to know of his prophetic calling by the power of the Holy Ghost; but I can raise some questions for him and other critics to deal with before they can dismiss Joseph Smith as a false prophet. I have time for only three of many that might be asked: first, what do you do with the Book of Mormon? second, how do you explain his power to influence strong men to follow him, even unto death? and third, how do you rationalize the fulfillment of his prophecies?

Here is the Book of Mormon. I hold it in my hand. I read its words. I have read Joseph Smith's explanation of how it came to be. To the unbelieving it is a story difficult to accept, and critics by the score have worn out their lives writing books intended to refute that story and to offer explanations other than the one given by Joseph Smith. But their critical writing only has the effect of stimulating scholars to dig the deeper, and the more deeply they dig the greater the accumulation of evidence for the validity of the story.

For instance, I have been fascinated with the recent studies of Dr. Alvin C. Rencher of this campus and Dr. Wayne A. Larsen of the Eyring Research Center on the "wordprints" of different authors in the Book of Mormon. They and others have demonstrated that just as a man's fingerprints are peculiar to him alone, so each author has word patterns that are peculiarly his. Presumably, if Joseph Smith, Sidney Rigdon, Solomon Spaulding, or any other one man wrote the Book of Mormon its language style would be the same in all of its books. But now, with computer technology, these scholars are led to conclude that statistically "the odds against a single author for the Book of Mormon exceed 100 billion to one" (Marc Haddock, "Computer Wordprints Track Writer's Style," *BYU Today*, November 1979, p. 1). Think of it. They further say: "All of our data point to one almost inescapable conclusion: No one man wrote the Book of Mormon. It seems impossible that Joseph Smith or any other writer, however brilliant, could have fabricated a work with 24 or more discernible wordprints." (Wayne A. Larsen, Alvin C. Rencher, and Tim Layton, "Multiple Authorship of the Book of Mormon," *New Era*, November 1979, p. 13.)

Joseph Smith did not write the Book of Mormon. Rather, "by the gift and power of God" (Book of Mormon, title page) he translated the writings of many authors who wrote at different times and under various circumstances.

This "wordprint" evidence, made possible through the modern computer, is to me remarkable and greatly appreciated. It significantly supplements a great and growing body of evidence for the validity of this remarkable book and for the man who was the instrument in the hands of God in bringing it forth "to the convincing of the Jew and Gentile that JESUS is the CHRIST" (Book of Mormon, title page).

As has been demonstrated for a hundred and fifty years, the truth of the book will not be determined by literary analysis or by scientific research, although these are reassuring and most welcome. The truth will be determined today and tomorrow, as it has been throughout the yesterdays, by the reading of it in a spirit of reverence and respect and prayer. I received a letter the other day from a father who said that, in response to the challenge I offered at general conference that we read the book again before next April, he and his family are going to read the first edition which touched so deeply so many strong and able men who read it when it first came from the press. I commended him but hastened to add that no one need look for a first edition to get the spirit of this remarkable volume. Every one of the million copies that will be printed this year carries that same spirit, includes that same marvelous promise, and will yield the same result in testimony concerning the truth of the book.

To return to my first question to the critics: What do you do with the Book of Mormon? It is here to be handled and to be read with prayer and earnest inquiry. All of the work of all of the critics throughout the hundred and fifty years of its presence has lacked credibility in the cold light of fact and has been without effect on those who have prayerfully read the book and received by the power of the Holy Ghost a witness of its truth. If there were no other evidence for the divine mission of Joseph Smith, the Book of Mormon would stand as an irrefutable witness of that fact. To think that anyone less than one inspired could bring forth a book which should have so profound an effect for good upon others is to imagine that which simply cannot be. The evidence for the truth of the Book of Mormon is found in the lives of the millions, living and gone, who have read it, prayed about it, and received a witness of its truth.

My second question to the critics: How do you explain Joseph's power to influence strong men and women to follow him, even unto death? Anyone who has any doubt about Joseph Smith's power of leadership need only look at the men who were attracted to him. They did not come for wealth. They did not come for political power. They were not drawn by dreams of military conquest. His offering to them was none of these; rather, it concerned only salvation through faith in the Lord Jesus Christ. It involved persecution with its pains and losses, long and lonely missions, separation from family and friends, and in many cases death itself.

Take, for instance, Orson Hyde, whose name has been much in Church news of late because of President Kimball's dedication of the memorial park on the Mount of Olives in Jerusalem. Orson Hyde was a clerk in the village of Kirtland when he met Joseph Smith, the youthful prophet. It was to this unknown, unpromising young seller of buttons and thread and calico that Joseph, speaking in the name of the Lord, said that he, Orson Hyde, was ordained "to proclaim the everlasting gospel, by the Spirit of the living God, from people to people, and from land to land, in the congregations of the wicked, in their synagogues, reasoning with and expounding all scriptures unto them" (D&C 68:1).

This young man, this clerk in a village store, under the inspiration of that prophetic call, walked two thousand miles on foot through Rhode Island, Massachusetts, Maine, and New York, "reasoning with and expounding all scriptures unto" all he met.

We were at the scene of his home in Nauvoo the other day, the comfortable home he left to travel to England and Germany and to visit Constantinople, Cairo, and Alexandria en route to Jerusalem where on October 24, 1841, he stood on the Mount of Olives and dedicated by the authority of the holy priesthood the land of Palestine for the return of the Jews. That was a quarter of a century before Herzl, the powerful exponent of Zionism, undertook the work of gathering the Jews to their homeland.

As another example, take Willard Richards—educated, refined, a doctor of medicine. When Joseph and Hyrum surrendered themselves to the governor of Illinois and were placed in Carthage Jail, a handful of the brethren went with them. By the afternoon of June 27, 1844, most had left to take care of certain matters of business, leaving only John Taylor and Willard Richards with the Prophet and his brother Hyrum. That afternoon following dinner the jailer, knowing of the mob outside, suggested that they would be safer in the cell of the jail. Turning to Willard Richards, Joseph asked, "If we go into the cell will you go with us?" To this Elder Richards responded:

> Brother Joseph, you did not ask me to cross the river with you—you did not ask me to come to Carthage—you did not ask me to come to jail with you—and do you think I would forsake you now? But I will tell you what I will do; if you are condemned to be hung for 'treason,' I will be hung in your stead, and you shall go free. [B.H. Roberts, *A Comprehensive History of the Church,* 2:283]

Strong and intelligent men do not demonstrate that kind of love for a charlatan or a fraud. That kind of love comes of God and the recognition of integrity in men. It is an expression of the spirit and example of the Savior, who gave his life for all men and who declared,

"Greater love hath no man than this, that a man lay down his life for his friends" (John 15:13).

If there were time we might speak of the others, so many of them—the Youngs, the Kimballs, the Taylors, the Snows, the Pratts, and their kind—who when they first met Joseph Smith were ordinary and unpromising in their appearance and ways, but who under his matchless energizing power became giants in achievement and immortal through their service to others.

Question three to the critics: What of his prophecies? There were more than a few, and they were fulfilled. Among the most notable was the revelation of the Civil War. You are familiar with it; it was spoken on Christmas Day, 1832. There were many high-minded men and women who deplored the institution of slavery then common in the South, and there was much talk of abolition. But who but a prophet of God would have dared to say, thirty-nine years before it was to happen that "war [would]be poured out upon all nations beginning at the rebellion of South Carolina" and that "the Southern States [would]be divided against the Northern States"? (D&C 87:1-3.) That remarkable prediction saw its fulfillment with the firing on Fort Sumter in Charleston Harbor in 1861. How could Joseph Smith have possibly foreseen with such accuracy the event that was to come thirty-nine years after he spoke of it. Only by the spirit of prophecy which was in him.

Or again, consider the equally remarkable prophecy concerning the movement of our people to these mountain valleys. The Saints were then living in Nauvoo and its sister community across the Mississippi and were enjoying a prosperity they had not previously known. They were building a temple and other substantial structures. Their new homes were of brick, constructed to endure. And yet one day in August of 1842, while visiting in Montrose, Joseph

prophesied that the Saints would continue to suffer much affliction and would be driven to the Rocky Mountains, many would apostatize, others would be put to death by our persecutors or lose their lives in consequence of exposure or disease, and [speaking to those who were present] some of you will live to go and assist in making settlements and build cities and see

the Saints become a mighty people in the midst of the Rocky Mountains.
[*History of the Church*, 5:85–86]

Viewed in the context of the time and circumstances, this statement is nothing less than remarkable. Only a man speaking with a knowledge beyond his own could have uttered words which would be so literally fulfilled, as your presence here tonight attests.

Great was his vision. It encompassed all the peoples of mankind, wherever they live, and all generations who have walked the earth and passed on. How can his critics, past or present, speak against him except out of ignorance? They have not tasted of his words; they have not pondered him and prayed about him. As one who has done these things, I can echo the words of John Taylor who was with him at Carthage Jail when he was killed and who in his account of that tragedy wrote this appraisal: "Joseph Smith, the Prophet and Seer of the Lord, has done more, save Jesus only, for the salvation of men in this world, than any other man that ever lived in it" (D&C 135:3).

To these I add my own words of testimony that he was and is a prophet of God, raised up as an instrument in the hands of the Almighty to usher in a new and final gospel dispensation. May I leave you with this quotation:

> *When a man gives his life for the cause he has advocated, he meets the highest test of his honesty and sincerity that his own or any future generation can in fairness ask. When he dies for the testimony he has borne, all malicious tongues should ever after be silent, and all voices hushed in reverence before a sacrifice so complete.* [Ezra Dalby, speech given December 12, 1926]

> *Great is his glory and endless his priesthood:*
> *Ever and ever the keys he will hold.*
> *Faithful and true, he will enter his kingdom,*
> *Crowned in the midst of the prophets of old.*
> ["Praise to the Man," *Hymns*, no.147]

In the name of Jesus Christ. Amen.

"A Choice Seer"

Neal A. Maxwell

I am aware that my wise and gentle friend Elder David B. Haight spoke about the Prophet Joseph a month ago. Please bear with me, therefore, as I seek to place the spotlight on the Seer in yet a different way on this Easter Sunday, during which our rejoicing is made more resplendent by the revelations and translations concerning Jesus that came to us through Joseph.

My appreciation is expressed to President Jeffrey Holland, Dean Robert Matthews, Professors Hugh Nibley, Jack Welch, Truman Madsen, Richard Anderson, Dean Jessee, and others for sharing knowledge with me that has been so helpful. These men do their part to slow the process of my becoming intellectually arthritic.

THE PROPHET JOSEPH SMITH

Whenever we talk about the Prophet Joseph Smith, it is important to remember what he said of himself: "I never told you I was perfect; but there is no error in the revelations which I have taught" (*Teachings*, p. 368). He was a good man, but he was called by

Neal A. Maxwell was a member of the Quorum of the Twelve Apostles of The Church of Jesus Christ of Latter-day Saints when this fireside address was given at Brigham Young University on 30 March 1986. © *Intellectual Reserve, Inc.*

a perfect Lord, Jesus of Nazareth! Joseph received his first counsel from God the Father, "This is My Beloved Son. Hear Him!" (JS—H 1:17). Joseph Smith listened carefully to Jesus then and ever after.

Ages ago in the Great Council, Jesus was the prepared but meek volunteer. As the Father described the plan of salvation and the need for a Savior, it was Jesus who stepped forward and said humbly but courageously, "Here am I, send me" (Abraham 3:27; see also Moses 4:2). Never has anyone offered to do so much for so many with so few words!

It is through the Prophet Joseph Smith, whom the resurrected Jesus called, that we learn these things, and so much more, about Jesus—long before Bethlehem and well beyond Calvary. Whenever we speak of the Prophet Joseph Smith, therefore, it should be in reverent appreciation of the Lord who called him and whom Joseph served so well.

From Joseph Smith, one unlearned and untrained in theology, more printed pages of scripture have come down to us than from any other mortal—in fact, as President Holland has pointed out, more than the combined pages, as available at present, from Moses, Paul, Luke, and Mormon.

But it is not only a matter of impressive quantity, it is also a qualitative matter, since dazzling doctrines came through the Prophet, including key doctrines previously lost from the face of the earth, a loss that caused people to "stumble exceedingly" (1 Nephi 13:34). "Plain and precious" things, because of faulty transmission, were "kept back" or "taken away" (see 1 Nephi 13:34, 39–40), and thus do not appear in our treasured Holy Bible.

What came *through* Joseph Smith was *beyond* Joseph Smith, and it *stretched* him! In fact, the doctrines that came through that "choice seer" (2 Nephi 3:6–7) by translation or revelation, are often so light-intensive that, like radioactive materials, they must be handled with great care!

By the way, it appears that in the process of translating the Book of Mormon in the spring of 1829, Joseph was moving along at the rate of seven to ten current printed pages a day. This is but one illustration of how blessed that "choice seer" was. Although Joseph could translate the words of the Book of Mormon, "The learned shall not read them, for they have rejected them" refers to a mind-set that is with us to this day, belonging to more than Professor Anthon (see 2 Nephi 27:20 and JS—H 1:64–65). In contrast, among an increasing number of mortals, Joseph is, as foreseen, "esteemed highly" (2 Nephi 3:7).

In 1833 Joseph was told not only that Jesus was with God premortally, but that:

Man was also in the beginning with God. Intelligence, or the light of truth, was not created or made, neither indeed can be. [D&C 93:29]

What a stunning parting of the curtains so that man could have a correct view of himself! The silence of centuries was officially broken. As the morning of the Restoration began to break, the shadows of false doctrines began to flee. Man's view of himself could become clearer, unimpeded by the overhanging of "original sin." We are accountable to a just God for our actual and individual sins—not for Adam's original transgression.

And the Lord said unto Adam: Behold I have forgiven thee thy transgression in the Garden of Eden.

Hence came the saying abroad among the people, that the Son of God hath atoned for original guilt, wherein the sins of the parents cannot be answered upon the heads of the children, for they are whole from the foundation of the world. [Moses 6:53–54; see also D&C 93:38 and Articles of Faith 1:2]

A stretching view of the universe was also made possible. Note what accompanied a wondrous witnessing of the resurrected Jesus:

For we saw him, even on the right hand of God; and we heard the voice bearing record that he is the Only Begotten of the Father—

That by him, and through him, and of him, the worlds are and were created, and the inhabitants thereof are begotten sons and daughters unto God. [D&C 76:23–24]

In June 1830 came "this precious morsel," which expands our perspective about this planet, described by Maimonides as "a speck among the worlds" (see Hugh Nibley, *Old Testament and Related Studies* [Salt Lake City: Deseret Book, 1986], p.139).

And worlds without number have I created; and I also created them for mine own purpose; and by the Son I created them, which is mine Only Begotten. . . .
    For behold, this is my work and my glory—to bring to pass the immortality and eternal life of man. [Moses 1:33, 39]

Even as our view of the universe was greatly enlarged, our view of human history was made much more intimate and familial:

Three years previous to the death of Adam, he called . . . the residue of his posterity who were righteous, into the valley of Adam-ondi-Ahman, and there bestowed upon them his last blessing.
    And the Lord appeared unto them, and they rose up and blessed Adam, and called him Michael, the prince, the archangel.
    And the Lord administered comfort unto Adam, and said unto him: I have set thee to be at the head; a multitude of nations shall come of thee, and thou art a prince over them forever.
    And Adam stood up in the midst of the congregation; and, notwithstanding he was bowed down with age, being full of the Holy Ghost, predicted whatsoever should befall his posterity unto the latest generation.
    These things were all written in the book of Enoch, and are to be testified of in due time. [D&C 107:53–57]

This startling and informing revelation came, by the way, in the midst of verses otherwise concerned with chronologies, genealogies, and duties.

Let others, if they choose, make jokes about our first parents, Adam and Eve, or regard them as mere myths. As a result of the Prophet Joseph Smith's revelations, we are blessed to know much more about "things as they really were, are, and will be" (see Jacob 4:13 and D&C 93:24)!

Latter-day Saints expectantly await the book of Enoch as being among the "many great and important things pertaining to the Kingdom of God" that God "will yet reveal" (Articles of Faith 1:9). As Professor Robert Matthews has observed, through Joseph Smith we received eighteen times as much as is in the Bible concerning Enoch. Without the Restoration, we would not even know there was a City of Enoch!

While others wonder if their mortal existence is absurd and pointless, we know otherwise about God's purposes, which he described before declaring, "This is the plan of salvation unto all men" (Moses 6:57–63). The process is a stern test:

And we will prove them herewith, to see if they will do all things whatsoever the Lord their God shall command them. [Abraham 3:25]

Nevertheless the Lord seeth fit to chasten his people; yea, he trieth their patience and their faith. [Mosiah 23:21]

How marvelous it is that these and so many other precious truths, just as prophesied, are "had again" among the children of men (Moses 1:41). No wonder there can and should be times for openly *enjoying* the faith as well as *defending* the faith.

These restored truths came fully formed. Joseph Smith did not receive such truths through Solomon Spaulding, Ethan Smith, Sidney Rigdon, Oliver Cowdery, or any others to be advanced by those desperate for any explanation other than the correct one. In 1850 Joseph's devoted helper, Phineas Young, wrote to Brigham Young in praise of Oliver Cowdery. Phineas wrote that the rebaptized Oliver Cowdery was now dead, but no one should forget his last testimony in which he said of Church headquarters in the West, "There was no salvation but in the valley and through the priesthood there." Oliver knew the source of the truths and priesthood which were restored through Joseph and the later *locus* of the presiding priesthood power. (see Phineas Young to Brigham Young, April 25, 1850, Brigham Young Collection, Historical Department, The Church of Jesus Christ of Latter-day Saints)

There is a legal doctrine meaning "the thing speaks for itself." The Everest of ecclesiastical truth built from the translations and revelations of the Prophet Joseph Smith speaks for itself as it towers above the foothills of philosophy. Even so, most will ignore it. Still others will reject the Restoration, supplying their own alternative explanations, just as some did who once heard thunder instead of the voice of God (see John 12:27–30). However, in a happy day ahead, "They that murmured shall learn doctrine" (Isaiah 29:24; 2 Nephi 27:35). This suggests that doctrinal illiteracy is a significant cause of murmuring among Church members.

The Restoration responds resoundingly and reassuringly to the key human questions and provides the firm framework of our faith. Do we actually live in an unexplained and unexplainable universe? Is there really purpose and meaning to human existence? Why such unevenness in the human condition? Why so much human suffering?

The marvelous truths of the Restoration respond to these questions and are highly global, highly personal, and even galactic in their dimensions! Identity exists amid immensity. We are enclosed in divine purposes! There is no need for despair! No wonder the restored gospel is such "good news."

These and other revelations came to us through an inspired prophet, Joseph Smith. His spelling left something to be desired, but how he provided us with the essential grammar of the gospel!

THE RESTORATION

Our present appreciation of the restored gospel lags embarrassingly far behind the stretching significance of its doctrines and theology. So far as our exploring the terrain of truth opened up to us by the Prophet Joseph is concerned, we have barely reached the Platte River, and it is time for us as a people to move on!

The Prophet is that "choice seer" of whom ancient Joseph spoke (2 Nephi 3:6–11), a major spiritual benefactor of the world. His salvational impact ultimately will be enormous, as the demographics of this dispensation alone assure (see D&C 135:3).

Like another prophet, Joseph served "notwithstanding [his] weakness" (2 Nephi 33:11). "Out of [Joseph's] weakness he [was] made strong" (2 Nephi 3:13). At one point, when he was translating the fourth chapter of 1 Nephi, Emma was acting as his scribe. Joseph reportedly encountered the words about the wall around Jerusalem (see 1 Nephi 4:5). He apparently paused and asked Emma if, in fact, there was a wall around Jerusalem. She replied in the affirmative. Joseph hadn't known (see *The History of the Reorganized Church of Jesus Christ of Latter Day Saints*, 1896, reprint [Independence, Missouri: Board of Publication, 1967], 4:447). According to Emma, when she and Joseph were interrupted during his translating, Joseph would later resume on the very sentence from which he had left off (see *Saints Herald*, 1 October 1879, pp. 289–90; see also Parley P. Pratt, *Autobiography of Parley P. Pratt* [Salt Lake City: Deseret Book Co., 1938], p. 62).

We naturally would like to know about that process of translation. In October 1831, Joseph Smith was asked by his brother Hyrum, at a conference held in Orange, Ohio, to give a firsthand account concerning the coming forth of the Book of Mormon. The Prophet replied "that it was not intended to tell the world all the particulars of the coming forth of the Book of Mormon; and . . . it was not expedient for him to relate these things" (*HC* 1:220). Since Joseph, who knew the "particulars," chose not to describe them in detail then, we cannot presently be definitive about methodology. But we can and should savor the supernal substance of the revelations and translations, which combine to prove to the world "that the holy scriptures are true" (D&C 20: 11; see also 1 Nephi 13:39–40).

Joseph Smith's time and place was one of religious fervor: "Lo, here!" and "Lo, there!" is Christ (JS—H 1:5). Ours is an age when, instead, the historicity of Christ is increasingly questioned. This condition only increases the relevance of the Restoration with its affirmation of Jesus' reality and his resurrection.

While Jesus declared that the scriptures "testify" of him (John 5:39), he neither expected nor received much coverage in secular history. Therefore, it is no surprise for studious Christians to learn that the secular history of that meridian period is nearly silent about the ministry of Jesus. Three secular writers, each writing after Jesus' crucifixion, touched slightly upon Christ. Tacitus (about A.D. 55–117), thought by many to be the greatest Roman historian, wrote only this: "Christus . . . had undergone the death penalty in the reign of Tiberius, by sentence of the procurator Pontius Pilatus" (*Annals of Tacitus* 15:44).

Suetonius (about A.D. 70–140), a Roman who wrote about the lives of various Caesars, called Jesus "Chrestus" and provided a sentence linking Chrestus to civil disturbance. Yet even this brief mention may contain a possible chronological error. (see *The Lives of the Caesars*, trans. J. C. Rolfe [Cambridge, Massachusetts: Harvard University Press, 1914], 5:51–52).

Josephus (about A.D. 37–95), in his *Antiquities*, wrote a few lines about the founder of Christianity, but later interpolations may cloud his meager lines (see, for example, 18:3). How important it is, given these conditions, that the New Testament not stand alone as evidence for Christ!

Joseph Smith was also an eyewitness of the resurrected Christ. Yet, as with all true disciples, Joseph went through a process of *proving, reproving,* and *improving,* while simultaneously serving as the human conduit through whom God chose to give his word to this generation (D&C 5:10).

The period of adversity commencing in Richmond Jail and continuing in Liberty Jail from 1 December 1838 until the first week in April 1839 provides a special window through which we can see the process of revelation and personal consolidation under way. Elder B. H. Roberts called the jail the "prison temple" (B. H. Roberts, *A Comprehensive History of the Church* [Salt Lake City, Utah: The Church

of Jesus Christ of Latter-day Saints, 1930], 1:526). Ironically, this
period of enforced idleness, grim though the conditions were, was
perhaps the only time in the Prophet's often hectic adult life when
there was much time for reflection.

The dungeon at Liberty Jail had inner and outer walls which,
combined, were four feet thick. Loose rocks were placed between the
walls to thwart any attempt at burrowing through. Unjustly arrested
and unjustly confined, Joseph and his companions tried twice to escape
but failed. As thick as those walls and that door were, and as securely
as they kept the Prophet and his fellow prisoners in, the walls were not
thick enough to keep revelation out!

During his stay in Liberty Jail, the Prophet Joseph Smith received
some of the most sublime revelations ever received by any prophet in
any dispensation, known now as sections 121 and 122 of the Doctrine
and Covenants. Therein are divine tutorials by which the Lord
schooled his latter-day prophet—probably the most tender tutorials in
all of holy writ now available.

A SPECIAL RELATIONSHIP

Joseph Smith was probably first made intellectually aware of the
special relationship he had with ancient Joseph, whom we commonly
refer to as Joseph in Egypt, when the Prophet Joseph translated the
third chapter of 2 Nephi. It was not until Liberty Jail, however, that
the record indicates any public affirmation of this unusual relationship. In one of his last letters from Liberty Jail, Joseph wrote, "I feel
like Joseph in Egypt" (*The Personal Writings of Joseph Smith*, comp.
Dean C. Jessee [Salt Lake City: Deseret Book, 1984], p. 409). It was
not an idle comparison, for it reflected an important verse in the
third chapter of 2 Nephi. Ancient Joseph spoke of the latter-day seer,
saying, "And he shall be like unto me" (2 Nephi 3:15).

When Joseph Smith, Jr., was given a blessing by Father Smith in
December 1834, an extensive portion of that blessing informed modern Joseph of his special relationship to ancient Joseph (see Joseph
Smith, Sr., blessing, 9 Dec. 1934, Church Historical Department,
1:3–4).

The comparisons between the two Josephs, of course, reflect varying degrees of exactitude, but they are, nevertheless, quite striking. Some similarities are situational, others are dispositional. Some are strategic, such as ancient Joseph's making stored grain available in time of famine (see Genesis 41:56), while modern Joseph opened the granary of the gospel after years of famine.

First, both Josephs had inauspicious beginnings. Initially, they were unlikely candidates to have had the impact they did on Egyptian history and American history, respectively.

Both had visions at a young and tender age (see Genesis 37:2–5 and JS—H 1). The visions brought to both men hate from their fellowmen (see Genesis 37:5–8 and JS—H 1:21–26). Both knew sibling jealousy. Modern Joseph had to contend with a mercurial brother, William, whom Joseph forgave many times (see HC 2:353–54).

Both Josephs were generous to those who betrayed them. Ancient Joseph was generous to his once-betraying brothers whom he later saved from starvation (see Genesis 45:1–15).

Both prophesied remarkably of the future of their nations and the challenges their governments would face (see Genesis 41:29–31 and D&C 87).

They both knew what it was to be falsely accused, and they both were jailed.

Both, in their extremities, helped others who shared their imprisonment, but who later forgot their benefactors. In the case of ancient Joseph, it was the chief butler (see Genesis 40:20–23). Joseph Smith worried over an ill cell mate, Sidney Rigdon, who was freed in January 1839. The Prophet rejoiced. Three months later, the Prophet inquired "after Elder Rigdon if he has not forgotten us" (*Writings*, p. 399).

Both Josephs were torn from their families, although ancient Joseph suffered through this for a much, much longer time.

Very significantly, both were "like unto" each other in being amazingly resilient in the midst of adversity. This, in each man, is a truly striking quality.

Both were understandably anxious about their loved ones and friends. Ancient Joseph, when his true identity became known, inquired tenderly of his brothers, "Doth my father yet live?" (Genesis 45:3). From Liberty Jail, the Prophet Joseph Smith, with comparative awareness, wrote, "Doth my friends yet live if they live do they remember me?" (*Writings*, p. 409).

Indeed, these two uncommon men had much in common, being truly "like unto" each other!

IN THE PRISON TEMPLE

The "prison temple" involved a time of obscurity, adversity, irony, and testimony. W. W. Phelps had briefly faltered, being part of the betrayals that had placed Joseph Smith in Liberty Jail. Joseph was, at the time, indignant over Brother Phelps' failures. Yet later on, Joseph was generous. The next year, 1840, when W. W. Phelps pled for readmission into the Church, Joseph Smith, who pledged from jail to act later "in the spirit of generosity," wrote a powerful and redemptive letter, the closing lines of which were, "Come on, dear brother, since the war is past, For friends at first, are friends again at last" (*HC* 4:164; see also pp. 162–63).

No wonder a grateful Brother Phelps, soon after Joseph's June 1844 martyrdom, wrote the text "Praise to the man who communed with Jehovah" (*Hymns*, 1985, no. 27).

The ironies in Liberty Jail are many. Though deprived of his constitutional rights, Joseph Smith therein praised the glorious U.S. Constitution. Then, after the misery of Missouri, Joseph declared with inspired anticipation:

I am willing to be sacrificed . . . maintaining the laws & Constitution of the United States if need be for the general good of mankind. [Andrew F. Ehat and Lyndon W. Cook, comps. and eds., *The Words of Joseph Smith* (Provo, Utah: Religious Studies Center, Brigham Young University, 1980), p. 320]

While being grossly abused by some biased political, judicial, and military leaders who wrongly used their powers Joseph received a glorious revelation. A sizable portion of that revelation, D&C 121, contrastingly sets forth the style and substance the Lord wants from his leaders that diverges so sharply from the ways of the world (see D&C 121:34–46).

Though Joseph was jailed nearly five months, more than four of these in Liberty Jail, he was told by the tutoring Lord that these things shall be "but for a small moment" (D&C 122:4; see also D&C 121:7). Though Joseph was suffering, the Lord reminded him that he was not suffering as much as Job had (see D&C 121:7–11). Only the Lord can compare crosses, and on that particular occasion he did (D&C 122:8).

The conditions in Liberty Jail were grim. The food was scanty and often consisted of leftovers from the jailer's table brought to them in a basket where chickens slept at night and which was often not cleaned. When the prisoners were permitted to cook, they had to endure smoke. It was also a particularly cold winter. The constant darkness bothered the prisoners' eyes. Joseph wrote about how his hand actually trembled as he penned his next-to-last letter to Emma (see *Writings*, p. 409).

In the midst of this stark obscurity and incessant difficulty, and with twelve thousand of Joseph's followers driven from the state of Missouri, the enemies of the Church probably felt that they had destroyed Joseph's work. Yet in the midst of all this deprivation, affliction, and obscurity, Joseph received the Lord's stunning assurance that "the ends of the earth shall inquire after thy name" (D&C 122:1).

How inspired and audacious a prophecy for any religious leader, let alone one on the obscure nineteenth-century American frontier. Meanwhile, Joseph's contemporary frontier and religious leaders have since become mere footnotes to history. But not Joseph!

Joseph, earlier in his imprisonment, had special assurances of which he later wrote,

Death stared me in the face, and . . . my destruction was determined upon, as far as man was concerned; yet, from my first entrance into the camp, . . . that still small voice, which has so often whispered consolation to my soul, in the depth of sorrow and distress, bade me be of good cheer, and promised deliverance, which gave me great comfort. [Writings (November 1839), p. 443]

However, Joseph was not unmindful or unaware of how grim things looked. With unusual empathy he observed from his prison temple: "Those who have persecuted us and smitten us and borne false witness against us . . . do seem to have a great triumph over us for the present"; then, "[But] Zion shall yet live though she seemeth to be dead" (*Writings*, pp. 375, 382).

It was from Liberty Jail that Joseph, more than once, testified that through God "we received the Book of Mormon" (*Writings*, p. 399), "that the Book of Mormon is true," and "that the ministering angels sent forth from God are true" (*Writings*, p. 407).

It was soon after his release from Liberty Jail that the Prophet Joseph Smith spoke about how the Book of Mormon was "the keystone of our religion" (*HC* 4:461).

After the Liberty Jail experience, the Prophet gave fervent public testimony about the Book of Mormon to a congregation of about three thousand in Philadelphia. When Sidney Rigdon, in his remarks on that same occasion, seemed to neglect the Book of Mormon in favor of citing the Bible, Joseph took the pulpit and declared, "If nobody else had the courage to testify of so glorious a message from Heaven, and of the finding of so glorious a record, he felt to do it" (*Words*, p. 45). The atmosphere, according to one present, was electric.

This is not to say that Joseph had not earlier been clear and declarative regarding the Book of Mormon. For instance, in an 1834 sermon, Joseph observed, "Take away the Book of Mormon and the revelations, and where is our religion?" (*Teachings*, p. 71).

Sharing the jail with Joseph was his brother Hyrum, ever faithful at Joseph's side. We have yet to pay Hyrum his due. Alas, we have little from his pen, but his actions spoke for him. However, on 16 March 1839, he wrote from Liberty Jail to a Sister Grinnal who was nursing Hyrum's wife, Mary Fielding, to his daughter, Lovina, and to a girl, Clarrinda. To Clarrinda he wrote:

> *Let mother give you one of the Books of Mormon & write your name in it. I want you to seek every opportunity to read it through. Remember me both night and morning in your prayers.*

To Lovina he wrote:

> *You may have my small Book of Mormon. You must try to read it through. Pray for your father that the Lord may help him to come home.* [Letter used with permission of Elder Eldred G. Smith, in whose possession it is.]

In the extremity of jail, Hyrum, so much at the center of things, joined Joseph in stressing the Book of Mormon.

Significantly, Joseph was released from the bondage of Liberty Jail 6 April 1839, and a few days later was allowed to escape from his captors. As you know, April 6 is the date of Jesus' birth. It is also the date of birth of his latter-day church (D&C 20:1). Additionally, the time of Joseph's release from the bondage of jail is often part of the season of Passover when our Jewish friends celebrate ancient Israel's deliverance and subsequent release from bondage in Egypt.

By the way, after Jesus' ascension when Herod "stretched forth his hands to vex certain of the church," he killed James, the brother of John, with a sword. When Herod saw the people's approval, he had Peter imprisoned, thinking to bring him to the people after Easter. But Peter was helped by the Lord to escape from prison during this same spring season (see Acts 12:1–5). Easter time is filled with rich remembrances.

The day the Prophet Joseph ended his bondage in Liberty Jail, 6 April 1839, involved yet another significant event. Heber C. Kimball recorded in his journal that on that day

the following words came to my mind, and the Spirit said unto me, "write,"
which I did by taking a piece of paper and writing on my knee as follows: . . .
"Verily I say unto my servant Heber, thou art my son, in whom I am well
pleased for thou art careful to hearken to my words, and not transgress my
law, nor rebel against my servant Joseph Smith, for thou has a respect to the
words of mine anointed, even from the least to the greatest of them; therefore
thy name is written in heaven, no more to be blotted out for ever, because of
these things." [*Words*, p. 18]

Note how much importance the Lord attached to our being loyal
to his servants! It is no different now.

With regard to the ministry of Joseph Smith, there are significant
expressions of divine determination. In each of these examples, the
Lord issued his declarations using the word "shall." The books of
scripture that were to come through the "choice seer" "*shall* grow
together" (2 Nephi 3:11–12; emphasis added). The books of scripture that came through Joseph Smith are joined with the Holy Bible,
especially now with the new recent publication of the four standard
works.

Another promise was given in the same chapter: those who would
try to destroy the work of the latter-day seer "*shall* be confounded"
(2 Nephi 3:14; emphasis added). This promise continues to be kept.

Joseph also received another *shall* promise, which likewise has
never been revoked: "Thy people *shall* never be turned against thee
by the testimony of traitors" (D&C 122:3; emphasis added). This
continues to be true today.

Furthermore, the central tutorial theme in Liberty Jail was also a
promise: "All these things *shall* give thee experience, and *shall* be for
thy good" (D&C 122:7; emphasis added).

Joseph Smith, Jr., was that "choice seer!" All the "shall" promises
about him shall be fulfilled, as the "ends of the earth shall inquire
after [his] name" (D&C 122:1).

A CHOICE SEER

Brigham Young, who was not easily impressed by anyone, observed that before he met Joseph Smith, he was searching for just such a seer:

The secret feeling of my heart was that I would be willing to crawl around the earth on my hands and knees, to see such a man as was Peter, Jeremiah, Moses, or any man that could tell me anything about God and heaven. . . .

. . . When I saw Joseph Smith, he took heaven, figuratively speaking, and brought it down to earth; and he took the earth, brought it up, and opened up, in plainness and simplicity, the things of God; and that is the beauty of his mission. [*JD* 8:228, 5:332]

On another occasion, Brigham said, "I feel like shouting hallelujah, all the time, when I think that I ever knew Joseph Smith" (*JD* 3:51). Significantly, Brigham's last mortal words were, "Joseph! Joseph! Joseph!" (Leonard J. Arrington, *Brigham Young: American Moses* [New York: Alfred A. Knopf, 1985], p. 399).

We have obligations to the Lord's prophets, past and present, which include being fair, posthumously or presently, concerning their words. The "choice seer," Joseph, reminded the Church in an epistle (December 1838) from jail that, "our light speeches from time to time . . . have nothing to do with the fixed principle of our hearts" (*Writings*, p. 376). Should we not distinguish between the utterances of the moment and considered opinions? Do not all of us wish for that same understanding on the part of our friends, hoping they, "with the breath of kindness," will "blow the chaff away"?

We are wise to follow, therefore, the example of Lorenzo Snow rather than that of Thomas B. Marsh. Marsh let himself become so preoccupied with the imperfections in the Prophet Joseph Smith that he found himself disaffected and out of the Church for a season. Lorenzo Snow said he had observed some imperfections in the Prophet Joseph Smith, but his reaction was that it was marvelous to see how the Lord could still use Joseph. Seeing this, Lorenzo Snow—

later President Snow—concluded that there might even be some hope for him!

One of the great messages that flows from the Lord's use of Joseph Smith as a "choice seer" in the latter days is that there is indeed hope for each of us! The Lord can call us in our weaknesses and yet magnify us for his purposes.

In the 1834 blessing, Father Smith promised Joseph, "Thou shalt fill up the measure of thy days" (Joseph Smith, Sr., blessing, pp. 3–4). The Lord likewise reassured the Prophet in Liberty Jail, "Thy days are known, and thy years shall not be numbered less" (D&C 122:9). It proved to be so. However, the Prophet was conscious of the pressures of time upon him. President Brigham Young, who visited Joseph in the prison temple, noted that Joseph told him, more than once, that he, Joseph, would not live to see his fortieth year *(Wilford Woodruff's Journal,* July 28, 1844 [Salt Lake City: Kraut's Pioneer Press, 1982]).

In the 1834 blessing, Joseph was promised that during his ministry, "Thy heart shall be enlarged" (Joseph Smith, Sr., blessing, pp. 3–4). An enlarged Joseph wrote from Liberty Jail,

It seems to me my heart will always be more tender after this than ever it was before . . . for my part I think I never could have felt as I now do if I had not suffered the wrongs that I have suffered. [Writings, pp. 386, 387]

In the 1834 blessing, the Prophet Joseph was promised, "Thou shalt like to do the work the Lord thy God shall command thee" (Joseph Smith, Sr., blessing, pp. 3–4). How often that intrinsic satisfaction sustained the Seer, when extrinsic conditions were so unsatisfactory!

On 4 April 1839, Joseph wrote his last letter to Emma from Liberty Jail "just as the sun [was] going down" while peeking through the "grates of this lonesome prison . . . with emotions known only to God" *(Writings,* p. 425). Such was Joseph's view of a temporal sunset that evening. But what a view of eternity he had and gave to us!

Joseph, as B. H. Roberts wrote, lived "in crescendo!" Looking back upon his busy, task-filled years, the Prophet said near the end,

"No man knows my history. I cannot tell it: I shall never undertake it. I don't blame anyone for not believing my history. If I had not experienced what I have, I would not have believed it myself" (*HC* 6:317). Thus, even in his adversity, Joseph had unusual empathy for those who lacked his special perspective.

This empathy extended beyond Joseph's own time and circumstances. He actually saw his prison sufferings as helping and expanding him "to understand the minds of the Ancients" *(Writings,* p. 387). A linkage was felt with their "afflictions," so that, said Joseph, "in the day of judgment . . . we may hold an even weight in the balances with them" *(Writings,* p. 395). How else could Joseph take his rightful place, "crowned in the midst of the prophets of old" (*Hymns;* 1985, no. 27)?

I gladly and gratefully testify that Joseph was and is a "choice seer," a prophet of God!

THE LORD AND HIS SERVANTS

Now may I close my message by bringing to the fore again, Jesus of Nazareth, who as the resurrected Lord and Savior called Joseph Smith. Let us focus on a particular part of the Atonement that makes the celebration of Easter possible.

A short while before Gethsemane and Calvary, Jesus prayed, "Now is my soul troubled; and what shall I say? Father, save me from this hour." Then, as if in soliloquy, he said, "But for this cause came I unto this hour" (John 12:27). The awful weight of the Atonement had begun to descend upon him. We next find him in Gethsemane.

And they came to a place which was named Gethsemane: and he saith to his disciples, Sit ye here, while I shall pray.

And he taketh with him Peter and James and John, and began to be sore amazed, and to be very heavy. [Mark 14:32–33]

The Greek for "very heavy" is "depressed, dejected, in anguish." Just as the Psalmist had foreseen, the Savior was "full of heaviness"

(Psalms 69:20). The heavy weight of the sins of all mankind were falling upon him.

He had been intellectually and otherwise prepared from ages past for this task. He is the creator of this and other worlds. He knew the plan of salvation. He knew this is what it would come to. But when it happened, it was so much worse than even he had imagined!

Now, brothers and sisters, this was not theater; it was the real thing. "And he went forward a little, and fell on the ground, and prayed that, if it were possible, the hour might pass from him" (Mark 14:35). Only in the Gospel of Mark do we get this next special pleading, "And he said, Abba, Father, all things are possible unto thee; take away this cup from me" (Mark 14:36). When Jesus used the word "Abba," it was a most personal and intimate familiar reference—the cry of a child in deepest distress for his father to help him in the midst of this agony.

Did Jesus hope there might be, as with Abraham, a ram in the thicket? We do not know, but the agony and the extremity were great. The sins and the grossness of all mankind were falling upon someone who was perfectly sinless, perfectly sensitive. This pleading to the Father included the doctrine he had taught in his ministry as Jehovah to Abraham and Sarah. "Is anything too hard for the Lord?" (Genesis 18:14). He had taught it in his mortal messiahship: "All things are possible to him that believeth" (Mark 9:23). Hence, this resounding plea. And then came that marvelous spiritual submissiveness: "Nevertheless not what I will, but what thou wilt" (Mark 14:36).

Luke wrote that at a particular point, an angel appeared to strengthen him. I do not know who that angel was, but what a great privilege to be at the side of the Son of God as he worked out the Atonement for the whole human family!

Jesus bled at every pore, and the bleeding started in Gethsemane. He was stretched to the limits. Later, when Jesus was on the cross, the Father, for reasons that are not completely apparent, withdrew his immediate presence from his son. The full weight fell upon him one last time, and there came the great soul cry, "My God, my God, why hast thou forsaken me?" (Mark 15:34).

Through that marvelous Prophet Joseph, in the book of Alma, we learned that Jesus not only suffered for our sins, but, in order to perfect his capacity of mercy and empathy, he also bore our sicknesses and infirmities that he might know "according to the flesh" (see Alma 7:11–12) what we pass through and thus become the perfect shepherd, which he is.

This is Jesus' Church, and Joseph was his prophet, and all the prophecies pertaining to his second coming will be fulfilled just as surely as all pertaining to his birth and early ministry were fulfilled.

He is our Lord, he is our God, and the day will come, brothers and sisters, when the veil will be stripped away, and you and I will see the incredible, spiritual intimacy that prevails between the Lord and his servants. Moses in the Sinai before the Exodus was on an exceedingly high mountain with Jesus—Jehovah. Not many centuries later, on the Mount of Transfiguration, Moses was again with his Lord and Savior, Jesus Christ. Someday we will see the interlacings of the lives of the Lord, his prophets, and our own. It is all part of Father in Heaven's glorious and wondrous plan of salvation—about which we know so much that matters through that remarkable Prophet Joseph Smith.

Praise to the man who communed with Jehovah! Praise to Jehovah for loving us and leading us and atoning for us. Praise to God the Father. Whenever we learn finally to love him, we must remember that he loved us first. Out of his love he has given to us this remarkable plan of salvation.

May God send us on our way with hearts brimming with joy for what we know. May we search the scriptures, follow their commandments, and rejoice in them. This is my prayer for myself and for you on this Easter evening, in the name of Jesus Christ. Amen.

Joseph Smith: A Revealer of Christ

Bruce R. McConkie

I devoutly and sincerely hope that we may have a rich outpouring of the Holy Spirit, for two reasons: first, so that I may say what the Lord wants said and what he would say if he personally were here; and secondly, so that those words will sink into your hearts and you will know of a surety that they are true. I shall take as a subject, "Joseph Smith: A Revealer of Christ."

I have chosen as a text statement these words, prepared and published by the First Presidency of the Church in 1935 on the occasion of the one hundredth anniversary of the organization of the first Quorum of Twelve Apostles in our dispensation:

Two great truths must be accepted by mankind if they shall save themselves: first, that Jesus is the Christ, the Messiah, the Only Begotten, the very Son of God, whose atoning blood and resurrection save us from the physical and spiritual death brought to us by the fall; and next, that God has restored to the earth, in these last days, through the Prophet Joseph Smith, His holy Priesthood with the fulness of the everlasting Gospel, for

Bruce R. McConkie was a member of the Quorum of the Twelve Apostles of The Church of Jesus Christ of Latter-day Saints when this fireside address was given at Brigham Young University on 3 September 1978. © Intellectual Reserve, Inc.

the salvation of all men on the earth. Without these truths man may not hope for the riches of the life hereafter. [The Improvement Era, April 1935, pp. 204–5]

We have a great pattern, a revealed pattern interwoven in all of the revelations that have been given in all ages, that indicates how salvation is made available to men on earth. As we are all aware, we are here on earth as the spirit children of God, our Heavenly Father. We are here inhabiting bodies—tabernacles made of clay—to be tried and examined and tested to see if we will do all things that the Lord directs and commands for his children generally and for each of us in particular. We are here to see if we will believe eternal truth and if we will conform to the principles so accepted and so learned. And if we believe and obey, we manage to do the things that will enable us, first, to have peace and joy and happiness in this life, and secondly, to go on to eternal reward in our Father's kingdom.

For every age in which the gospel is given, for every gospel dispensation, for every time that a gracious God dispenses the plan of salvation to his children on earth, he follows an identical pattern: he reveals two great truths which apply to the dispensation involved. One of these truths applies to all dispensations and the other to the specific dispensation. The truth of universal application for all men in all ages from father Adam to the last man is that salvation is in Christ; that he is the Redeemer and Savior of men; that in and through his atoning sacrifice, by the blood that he shed and the redemption that he wrought, salvation is available for all men. Because of Christ, all men will be raised in immortality, and those who believe and obey will then be raised unto eternal life in our Father's kingdom.

Immortality, by definition and in its nature, is to live everlast-ingly with a body of flesh and bones; it is to be resurrected; it is to have body and spirit inseparably connected. Eternal life, on the other hand, is, for one thing, to live eternally in the family unit and, for another thing, to inherit, possess, and receive the dignity, honor, power, and glory of God himself. Anyone for whom the family unit continues in eternity will have eternal life, and in process of time he will acquire all the dignity, honor, glory, power, might, and omnipotence that the Eternal Father possesses.

Immortality comes because of the Lord Jesus Christ; it is a free gift for all men. Eternal life is made available through the same atoning sacrifice, and it is a gift to all who obey the law upon which its receipt is predicated. The laws of salvation are the same for every age. They have never varied, and they will never vary. Every man from Adam to the last soul to inhabit this earth must do precisely and exactly the same things and obey the same laws in order to inherit, receive, and possess the same glory in eternity.

Salvation is in Christ, and in order for men to believe and obey, the laws of Christ and the doctrine of Christ—which comprise his everlasting gospel—must be revealed in whatever age is involved. That is a universal, unvarying requirement. The gospel did not originate in the meridian of time—it did not start when the Lord Jesus was upon earth. It is an everlasting gospel. It commenced in the beginning, it has come down in successive periods or dispensations from the days of Adam to the present, and it will continue as long as men are on earth; and always and everlastingly salvation will be in Christ.

But we need a revealer of the knowledge of salvation for whatever dispensation is involved. Our revelation says, "Salvation was, and is, and is to come, in and through the atoning blood of Christ, the Lord Omnipotent" (Mosiah 3:18). We need make no mistake about that. Our affection, our interest, our concern, our love, our devotion—all that we have and all that we possess is centered in the Lord Jesus; but, having said that affirmatively and unequivocally and positively, we come to the fact that a revealer of the knowledge of Christ and of salvation is needed for every age of the earth. Thus we find such a thing in our revelations as this: "Joseph Smith, the Prophet and Seer of the Lord, has done more, save Jesus only, for the salvation of men in this world, than any other man that ever lived in it" (D&C 135:3). And so, for our dispensation, we link the names of Christ and of Joseph Smith.

Now I read you these words of Brigham Young:

Who can justly say aught against Joseph Smith? I was as well acquainted with him, as any man. I do not believe that his father and mother knew him any better than I did. I do not think that a man lives on the earth that knew him any better than I did; and I am bold to say that, Jesus Christ excepted, no better man ever lived or does live upon this earth. I am his witness. He was persecuted for the same reason that any other righteous person has been or is persecuted at the present day. [John A. Widtsoe, comp., *Discourses of Brigham Young,* 2d ed., pp. 702–3]

Let us gain a true vision; let us reason together and figure out how the Lord operates with reference to his children. First of all, we read in the visions of Abraham about the noble and great in the premortal life who were foreordained. Abraham is told that he is one of them. They are identified as the offspring of the Father, as spirits, as souls; and then the account says, "And there stood one among them that was like unto God." This is the Lord Jesus, the Lord Jehovah. This is the firstborn in the spirit who, through righteousness and zealousness and obedience, became "like unto God," meaning unto the Father.

And he [that is, Christ] *said unto those who were with him* [the host of noble and great ones, the ones Abraham had seen]: *We will go down* [not I, Jehovah, alone, but we, the noble and great, the mighty and valiant sons of our Father; we will go down] *for there is space there, and we will take of these materials, and we will make an earth whereon these* [that is, the spirit hosts of heaven] *may dwell;*

And we will prove them herewith, to see if they will do all things whatsoever the Lord their God shall command them. [Abraham 3:24–25]

Who is listed and counted in that great council of eternity, that assemblage of the noble and great seen by Abraham? There is not much question in our minds; they were the people who were foreordained to minister to men in this world.

We know a little bit about the order of priority, the precedence, and the rank that is involved. We know that the Lord Jesus was number one: mighty, superior, valiant, intelligent above all others. We know that a spirit named Michael was number two, and that he was born into this world as Adam, the first man. We know that a spirit named Gabriel stood third in preeminence, might, and power, and that he came among us as Noah.

After that we cannot specifically and definitely categorize the various spirits; but we do know that the noblest and the greatest and the mightiest among them were ordained to be heads of dispensations—to be the individuals who, for their era and age and dispensation, would commence the spread of eternal truth on earth. We know, for instance, with reference to Moses, who was the head of one of these dispensations, that "there arose not another prophet . . . in Israel like unto Moses, whom the Lord knew face to face" (Deuteronomy 34:10). That sets us a pattern. We know of men like Enoch, who so lived that he perfected his whole city and his whole people, and they were translated and taken up into heaven. We look back at Abraham and consider him to be the Father of the Faithful and rejoice that we are born as his seed.

There is a limited number of mighty, noble spirits who headed the respective dispensations. How many we do not know; perhaps there were eight or ten or twenty, but the number does not matter. At any rate, we soon have a small group of select individuals who stand in intelligence and power and might next to the Lord Jehovah. In the same sense that he was like unto God, these chosen and select individuals who were destined to head his work for these long ages were like unto Christ.

When sifting out the relative importance of individuals, without knowing the details, we can conclude that a man born in modern times to head this dispensation was like unto Adam, like unto Moses, like unto Abraham, like unto Christ—in other words, was one of the ten or twenty noblest and greatest spirits who, up to this time, have been born into mortality. He and hosts with him performed their labors and their work in the creative enterprises that brought this earth rolling into existence, and he and his associates headed the periods of time when eternal truth went out to the sons of men.

That is how we rank and place the prophet Joseph Smith: he is one of the great dispensation heads, and a dispensation head is a revealer for his age and his period of the knowledge of Christ and of salvation. Thus, the other prophets of the dispensation who are associated with him and who come after him, who sustain his work and bear record of him, become witnesses that he—the chief prophet of their age—revealed the Lord Jesus and hence made salvation available.

This means that in a testimony meeting in our day we link the name of Joseph Smith with that of Jesus Christ. We stand up and say, "I know that Jesus Christ is the Son of the living God and that he was crucified for the sins of the world." And in the next breath we say, "I know that Joseph Smith, Junior, was chosen, appointed, anointed, and called as God's prophet for this age in order to reveal Christ and to reveal salvation." We bear witness of Christ, and we bear witness of Joseph Smith.

That is the way it has been from the beginning. There have always been testimony meetings. If we had lived in the days of Adam and had assembled to worship the Lord, the Spirit would have rested mightily upon us on occasions and we would have said, "I know that salvation is in Christ who shall come, and I know that Adam, our father, is a legal administrator who holds keys and powers and authority, and that he is the revealer of the knowledge of Christ and of salvation for men on earth."

If we had lived in the days of Enoch, we would have arisen in our testimony meetings and said, "I testify of Christ, and I testify of Enoch who revealed Christ, and automatically I believe also in Adam who went before." That pattern would also have been followed in Noah's day, in Abraham's day, in Melchizedek's day, and in every age when eternal truth has been revealed. Always we would have linked the name of Christ and the name of the dispensation head, and automatically we would have believed in every prophet that went before.

We cannot suppose for one minute that it would be possible for someone who lived in the days of the Lord Jesus to believe that he was the son of God and yet to reject the witness of Peter, James, and

John. That is a philosophical impossibility. Had we lived in that day it would not have been possible to say, "Well, I'll believe in Christ; but I won't believe in Peter, James, and John, his apostles, who have revealed him to me and who have borne witness of his divine Sonship." The Lord and his prophets always go together. With that in mind let me read these words of Brigham Young:

Whosoever confesseth that Joseph Smith was sent of God to reveal the holy Gospel to the children of men, and lay the foundation for gathering Israel, and building up the kingdom of God on the earth, that spirit is of God; and every spirit that does not confess that God has sent Joseph Smith, and revealed the everlasting Gospel to and through him, is of Antichrist, no matter whether it is found in a pulpit or on a throne. [JD 8:176–77]

Having these concepts and these expressions in mind, I am going to read to you some passages given and spoken by the Lord Jesus, in which he associates himself with John the Baptist. Out of these passages we shall have an affirmation and a reaffirmation of the truth and concept that Christ and his prophets go together, that it is not possible to believe in one without believing in the other, and that by rejecting the prophets we reject Christ himself. Jesus said this:

If I bear witness of myself, yet my witness is true.

For I am not alone, there is another who beareth witness of me, and I know that the testimony which he giveth of me is true.

Ye sent unto John, and he bare witness also unto the truth.

And he received not his testimony of man, but of God, and ye yourselves say that he is a prophet, therefore ye ought to receive his testimony. [John 5:32–35; Joseph Smith Translation of the Bible, hereafter cited as JST; all biblical references without this notation come from the King James Version]

John bore as persuasive and powerful a testimony as we know of or find in any written record. On those occasions of Christ's visits to him near Bethabara, as he baptized in Jordan, he said, "Behold the

Lamb of God, which taketh away the sin of the world" (John 1:29, 36). That was simply a text statement or a subject head for long discourses that he obviously preached about the divine Sonship. On one occasion John said this—and it is as blunt and as plain as any witness—"He that believeth on the Son hath everlasting life: and he that believeth not the Son shall not see life; but the wrath of God abideth on him" (John 3:36). John said, in effect, "Here is Jesus; he is the Son of God." There was no possible way to believe that John was a prophet and reject the Lord Jesus. To accept one was to accept the other. Jesus said,

> *John came unto you in the way of righteousness, and bore record of me, and ye believed him not; but the publicans and the harlots believed him; and ye, afterward, when ye had seen me, repented not, that ye might believe him.*
>
> *For he that believed not John concerning me, cannot believe me, except he first repent.*
>
> *And except ye repent, the preaching of John shall condemn you in the day of judgment.* [Matthew 21:32–34; JST]

We could recite that over again, paraphrasing the language, and apply it to Joseph Smith and his situation in our day.

Here is another passage:

> *Then said the Pharisees unto him, Why will ye not receive us with our baptism, seeing we keep the whole law?*
>
> *But Jesus said unto them, Ye keep not the law. If ye had kept the law, ye would have received me, for I am he who gave the law.*
>
> *I receive not you with your baptism, because it profiteth you nothing.*
>
> *For when that which is new is come, the old is ready to be put away.* [Matthew 9:18–21; JST]

Following those expressions came the ones with which we are so familiar, about putting new wine in old bottles. In other words, we have new revelation in our day in a new church, just as the case was in the meridian dispensation.

Then certain of them came to him, saying, Good Master, we have Moses and the prophets, and whosoever shall live by them, shall he not have life?

And Jesus answered, saying, Ye know not Moses, neither the prophets; for if ye had known them, ye would have believed on me; for to this intent they were written. For I am sent that ye might have life. [Luke 14:35–36; JST]

The principle that the Lord and his prophets go together is a glorious one. Here are some words I wrote on this subject on one occasion.

LIVING ORACLES

We be Abraham's children, the Jews said to Jove;
We shall follow our Father, inherit his trove.
But from Jesus our Lord, came the stinging rebuke:
Ye are children of him, whom ye list to obey;
Were ye Abraham's seed, ye would walk in his path,
And escape the strong chains of the father of wrath.

We have Moses the seer, and the prophets of old;
All their words we shall treasure as silver and gold.
But from Jesus our Lord, came the sobering voice;
If to Moses ye turn, then give heed to his word;
Only then can ye hope for rewards of great worth,
For he spake of my coming and labors on earth.

We have Peter and Paul, in their steps let us trod;
So religionists say, as they worship their God.
But speaks He who is Lord of the living and dead:
In the hands of those prophets, those teachers and seers,
Who abide in your day have I given the keys;
Unto them ye must turn, the Eternal to please.

With those principles in mind, let us be vividly and acutely aware of their application to Joseph Smith. One of our revelations says—in the words of the Lord Jesus, speaking to Joseph Smith—"This generation shall have my word through you" (D&C 5:10). I think He made that statement, either in those verbatim words or in thought content, to every dispensation head there has been. I think he said it to Enoch, Moses, Abraham, and in principle to all: "This generation shall have my word through you." Someone has to reveal eternal truth, and these brethren whom I have mentioned are the ones to whom the Lord gave that obligation.

Therefore, we find such directives as this, spoken by the Lord to the Church immediately following its organization on the sixth day of April in 1830. He is talking about Joseph Smith:

Thou [the church] *shalt give heed unto all his words and commandments which he shall give unto you as he receiveth them, walking in all holiness before me.*

[Now note:] *For his word ye shall receive, as if from mine own mouth, in all patience and faith.* [This sets a dispensation head apart from all other prophets. Here is the subsequent statement about him:]

Behold, I will bless all those who labor in my vineyard with a mighty blessing, and they shall believe on his words, which are given him through me by the Comforter, which manifesteth that Jesus was crucified by sinful men for the sins of the world, yea, for the remission of sins unto the contrite heart. [D&C 21:4–5, 9]

What is the measure of our discipleship? How do we measure and test how firmly we are rooted in the restored faith? I think one of the great tests is the degree and the extent, the fervor and sincerity, the devotion and true belief that we give to the words that came from the Prophet Joseph Smith. Here is a man that, first of all, gave us the Book of Mormon—the Book of Mormon, which is an account of God's dealings with a people who had the fullness of the gospel, which bears record of Christ, which recounts in plainness and in simplicity the basic and fundamental truths that men must believe to be saved. Here is a man who gave a book of incomparable value—his words, as it were to us, at least, because it was through his instrumentality that they came. Here is a man who gave us the revelations in the Doctrine and Covenants—revelations which speak in the first person, with the Lord Jesus himself being mouth and voice but the lips being the lips of Joseph Smith—a volume of revealed truth where God Almighty speaks through his prophet.

Here are words that the Prophet gave us in the Pearl of Great Price, the Book of Moses being taken from the Joseph Smith translation of the scriptures and the Book of Abraham being translated from the papyrus. Here are words in many places in the Joseph Smith Translation itself, revealed words that come from God by prophetic power. Here are sermons—majestic, wondrous, marvelous sermons which recount the mind and will and plan and purposes of the Lord to men on earth—for instance, the King Follet sermon from which President Kimball quoted copiously at the funeral sermon of Brother Stapley recently.

We speak about judging a man by his fruits, and among the great fruits of Joseph Smith are the words that he spoke, the words that he wrote, the inspired message that he gave. I suggest that a measure of discipleship, a standard of judgment whereby we can tell how firmly we are anchored in the faith of the Lord, is how sincerely and completely we believe the words that have come from the Prophet Joseph Smith. Obviously incident to this, we have an obligation and a need to treasure up these words, to search out these truths, to learn what they are, and then to make them a living part of us.

We bear testimony of Christ, and we do it with all the fervor and conviction and power of our whole soul, striving and laboring to do it by the power of the Holy Ghost; and as our voices echo and reecho the eternal verity that Christ is the Lord, we say also that Joseph Smith is a prophet of God, a legal administrator who had power from God—keys and authority—so that he could bind on earth and have it sealed eternally in the heavens. Here, we say, is Joseph Smith, a revealer of the knowledge of Christ and of salvation for our day. We link the words together in one great testimony of eternal truth; and the reason we have power to bear witness of Christ, through whom salvation comes, is that Joseph Smith, the prophet and seer of the

Lord for our day and in our day, has received eternal truth, has borne witness, has given revelation, has laid the foundation.

Brigham Young once said, "I feel like shouting Hallelujah, all the time, when I think that I ever knew Joseph Smith" (*Discourses of Brigham Young*, p. 458); and that is as it ought to be, because salvation is in Christ and salvation is available because Joseph Smith revealed Christ to the world. The world either accepts that witness and believes in the Lord's prophets or goes its way and at its peril loses the hope of eternal salvation. One must believe in Adam and Christ, if living in that day; or in Abraham and Christ, if living in that day; or in Moses and Christ if living then; or, in our day, in Joseph Smith and Jesus Christ, crying "Hosanna" and "Hallelujah" and "Praise the Lord" whenever their names are mentioned by the power of the Holy Spirit.

I am grateful beyond any measure of expression I have that in my soul there rests the absolute, certain conviction that Jesus is the Lord. I know that as well as I know anything in this world. In that same sense—with unshaken certainty and absolute, pure, revealed knowledge—I know that Joseph Smith, Junior, who headed this dispensation, as the Lord's prophet for our day and our time; and that, as he certified, he saw in the spring of 1820 the Father and the Son; and that, as he certified, the revelations and the truths that fell from his lips are the voice and mind and will and purposes of the Lord for me and for all men in our day.

I pray God our Father that we may be valiant and true, that we may stand affirmatively and courageously in bearing witness of Christ—because salvation is in Christ and in none other—and that we will have the same fervor and the same devotion in linking the mighty and noble name of the head of our dispensation with the name of the Savior himself.

This I do by way of doctrine and by way of testimony on this occasion in the name of the Lord Jesus Christ. Amen.

Joseph Smith
and the Problem of Evil

David L. Paulsen

Nothing challenges the rationality of our belief in God or tests our trust in Him more severely than human suffering and wickedness. Both are pervasive in our common experience. If this is not immediately evident, a glance at the morning paper or the evening news will make it so. On the larger scale and at the moment, names like Oklahoma City, Columbine, Kosovo, and Turkey evoke image upon image of unspeakable human cruelty or grief. But Auschwitz and Belsen still haunt our memories. Closer to home, who can fathom the anguish of family members in West Valley when they discovered their precious little girls suffocated together in the trunk of an automobile, the tragic outcome of an innocent game of hide-and-seek. Or the trauma of a dear friend of mine and his five young children who day by day for several months watched their lovely wife and mother wither down to an emaciated skeleton of 85 pounds as she endured a slow and painful death from inoperable cancer of the throat. Scenes like these are repeated daily a thousand and a thousand times.

David L. Paulsen was a BYU professor of philosophy when this forum address was given on 21 September 1999. © Brigham Young University.

But we need not speak only of the sufferings of others. Few of us here will escape deep anguish, for it is apparently no respecter of persons and comes in many guises, arising out of our experiences of incurable or debilitating diseases, mental illness, broken homes, child and spouse abuse, rape, wayward loved ones, tragic accidents, untimely death—the list goes on and on. No doubt many of us have already cried out, "Why God? Why?" And many of us, often on behalf of a loved one, have already pleaded, "Please, God, please help," and then wondered as, seemingly, the only response we've heard has been a deafening silence. All of us have struggled, or likely will struggle, in a very personal way with the problem of evil.[1]

I say *the* problem of evil, but actually there are many. Today I want to consider with you just three, which I will call (1) the logical problem of evil; (2) the soteriological problem of evil; and (3) the practical problem of evil. The logical problem is the apparent contradiction between the world's evils and an all-loving, all-powerful Creator. The soteriological problem is the apparent contradiction between certain Christian concepts of salvation and an all-loving Heavenly Father. The practical problem is the challenge of living trustingly and faithfully in the face of what personally seems to be overwhelming evil.

I. THE LOGICAL PROBLEM OF EVIL

Soaked as it is with human suffering and moral evil, how is it *possible* that our world is the work of an almighty, perfectly loving Creator? So stated, the logical problem of evil poses a puzzle of deep complexity. But the conundrum evoked by our reflection on this question appears to be more than just a paradox: we seem to stare contradiction right in the face. The ancient philosopher Epicurus framed the contradiction in the form of a logical dilemma: Either God is unwilling to prevent evil or He is unable. If He is unwilling, then He cannot be perfectly good; if He is unable, then He cannot be all powerful. Whence then evil? And 18th-century sceptic David Hume expressed the contradiction in much the same way:

Why is there any misery at all in the world? Not by chance, surely. From
some cause then. Is it from the intention of the Deity? But he is perfectly
benevolent. Is it contrary to his intention? But he is almighty. Nothing can
shake the solidity of this reasoning, so short, so clear, so decisive.[2]

Hume's succinct statement has since provided the framework
within which the logical problem of evil has been discussed. However,
I believe Hume's way of formulating the problem is far too narrow,
unjust to both challenger and defender of belief in God—especially
to the Christian defender. I do not believe that for the challenger
intent on disproving God's existence the problem has been stated in
its starkest terms. For in addition to affirming that (i) God is perfectly
good and (ii) all powerful, traditional Christian theologians commonly
affirm two additional propositions that intensify the problem: (iii) God
created all things absolutely—that is, out of nothing; and (iv) God has
absolute foreknowledge of all the outcomes of His creative choices.
Although apologists for belief in God have labored long to reconcile
the world's evil with God's goodness and power, they have often over-
looked the much more difficult task of reconciling evil not only with
His goodness and power but with God's absolute creation and absolute foreknowledge as well. Twentieth-century English philosopher
Antony Flew takes these additional premises into account in arguing
that any such reconciliation is impossible. It is perfectly proper in the
face of apparently pointless evil, he says, to look first for some *saving*
explanation that will show that, in spite of appearances, there really is
a God who loves us. But Flew claims that believers have assigned God
attributes that block a saving explanation altogether:

We cannot say that [God] *would like to help but cannot: God is omnipotent.*
We cannot say that he would help if he only knew: God is omniscient. We
cannot say that he is not responsible for the wickedness of others: God creates
those others. Indeed an omnipotent, omniscient God must be an accessory
before (and during) the fact to every human misdeed; as well as being
responsible for every non-moral defect in the universe.[3]

To state Flew's argument differently: If God creates all things (including finite agents) absolutely (that is, out of nothing), knowing beforehand all the actual future consequences of His creative choices, then He is an accessory before the fact and ultimately responsible for every moral and nonmoral defect in the universe. And if, as some believers allege, some human agents will suffer endlessly in hell, God is also at least jointly responsible for these horrendous outcomes. But if so, how can He possibly be perfectly loving? Given the traditional understanding of God, whatever our consistency-saving strategies, in the end, I believe, we must candidly confess that they are not very convincing.

On the other hand, this exclusive focus on reconciling evil with *just* a set of divine attributes is unfair to the Christian defender. For it fails to acknowledge the incarnation of God the Son in the person of Jesus of Nazareth and His triumph over suffering, sin, and death through his atonement and resurrection. Any Christian account of the problem of evil that fails to consider this—Christ's mission to overcome the evil we experience—will be but a pale abstraction of what it could and should be.

I propose, then, to consider the problem of evil from this broader perspective, confronting it in terms of its starkest statement but also in terms of its strongest possible solution: a worldview centered in the saving acts of Jesus Christ.

The Prophet Joseph Smith received revealed insights that *do* address the problem of evil in its broadest terms. His revelations suggest what might be called a soul-making theodicy, centered within a distinctively Christian soteriology (or doctrine of salvation), but both framed within a theology that rejects both absolute creation and, consequently, the philosophical definition of divine omnipotence which affirms that there are no (or no nonlogical) limits to what God can do. The Prophet's worldview, I believe, dissolves the logical and soteriological problems of evil while infusing with meaning and hope our personal struggles with suffering, sin, and death. To show (albeit briefly) that this is so is my purpose this morning.

Theodicy (literally, God's justice) is the attempt to reconcile God's goodness with the evil that occurs in the world. In coming to appreciate the power of Joseph Smith's revealed insights for such reconciliation, it will be instructive to compare and contrast them with the theodicy developed by contemporary philosopher John Hick in his fine book *Evil and the God of Love*, widely recognized as the watershed work on the problem of evil.

In *Evil and the God of Love*, Hick constructs a soul-making theodicy that retains the doctrine of absolute creation. The soul-making component in Hick's theodicy is highly reminiscent of Joseph Smith's revelation. Both affirm that God's fundamental purposes in creating us and our world environment include first, enabling us, as morally and spiritually immature agents created in the image of God, to develop into God's likeness; and second, enabling us to enter into an authentic (that is, a free and uncompelled) relationship of love and fellowship with Him. To achieve these ends, Hick says, God endowed us with the power of self-determination (or, as he calls it, incompatibilist freedom) and, to preserve that freedom, epistemically distanced us from Himself. God effects that distancing, Hick suggests, by having us emerge as largely self-centered creatures out of a naturalistic evolutionary process; or, as Joseph Smith maintains, by God's "veiling" our memory of our premortal existence. God also endowed us, Hick says, with a rudimentary awareness of Him and some tendency toward moral self-transcendence. The Prophet identifies this awareness and predisposition as the light of Christ, or the Spirit, which "enlighteneth every man through the world" (D&C 84:46). Soul-making (that is, development into the moral and spiritual likeness of God) occurs as we overcome our self-centeredness by making moral choices within an environment fraught with hardship, pain, and suffering.

To this point, the understandings of Hick and Joseph Smith seem strikingly similar.

Absolute Creation: Hick and Joseph Smith

With respect to creation, however, Hick and the Prophet maintain decidedly different positions. Hick affirms absolute creation (or creation out of nothing), whereas Joseph Smith denies it. And this difference brings us to a major point of my address. With his affirmation of absolute creation, Hick affirms all four theological postulates—perfect goodness, absolute power, absolute foreknowledge, and absolute creation—which confront him head-on with Flew's divine complicity argument. And Hick sees as clearly as Flew, and explicitly acknowledges, the logical consequence of his position: God *is* ultimately responsible for *all* the evil that occurs in the world. Hick explains why this is so.

One whose action, A, is the primary and necessary precondition for a certain occurrence, O, all other direct conditions for O being contingent upon A, may be said to be responsible for O, if he performs A in awareness of its relation to O and if he is also aware that, given A, the subordinate conditions will be fulfilled. . . . [God's] *decision to create the existing universe was the primary and necessary precondition for the occurrence of evil, all other conditions being contingent upon this, and He took His decision in awareness of all that would flow from it.*[4]

But given Hick's admission that God is ultimately responsible for all the evil that occurs in the world, how can he possibly claim that God is perfectly loving?

Hick's Way Out

Hick sees one, and *only* one, way out. His avenue of escape is through an appeal to a doctrine of universal salvation. In Hick's view, all of us will finally achieve an authentic relationship with God in a postmortal life, the value of which will far outweigh any finite evil suffered here. He explains:

We must thus affirm in faith that there will in the final accounting be no personal life that is unperfected and no suffering that has not eventually become a phase in the fulfilment of God's good purpose. Only so, I suggest, is it possible to believe both in the perfect goodness of God and in His unlimited capacity to perform His will. For if there are finally wasted lives and

*finally unredeemed sufferings, either God is not perfect in love or He is not
sovereign in rule over His creation.*[5]

Though I find Hick's way out appealing, its scriptural warrant is
questionable, and it engenders conceptual difficulties of its own. Let
us consider briefly just two.

1. Though in Hick's view God endows us with a strong power of
self-determination, it does not follow from his view that our choices
occur in a vacuum. They are always choices of particular persons with
particular natures. Recall that Hick describes our primordial nature
as being largely self-centered with a rudimentary awareness of God
and some slight tendency toward morality. Since in Hick's account
God creates out of nothing these primal natures (or, alternatively, the
world process that invariably produces these natures), I see no reason,
given Hick's assumptions, why God could not have made us significantly better than we are. Why not, for example, give us some significant reduction in our sometimes seemingly overwhelming tendencies
to self-centeredness or some significant increase in our natural
aversion to violence? Such creative choices on God's part might have
narrowed somewhat the options over which our own choices might
range, but would apparently negate neither incompatibilist freedom
nor soul-making objectives. Seemingly, Hick's absolute creator could
have made a much better world than ours.

2. On the other hand, it is hard to see how it can be certain (as
Hick claims) that God, without compromising anyone's freedom, will
inevitably lure every finite agent into a loving relationship with himself. Given that in Hick's view we must have incompatibilist freedom
in order to enter into an authentic personal relationship with God,
how can it be certain that there won't be, as C. S. Lewis suggested,
"rebels to the end" with "the doors of hell . . . locked on the *inside*"?[6]
How can this possibility be precluded? Hick suggests that although it
is not theoretically, it is practically precluded because

*God has formed the free human person with a nature that can find its
perfect fulfilment and happiness only in active enjoyment of the infinite*

goodness of the Creator. He is not, then, trying to force or entice His creatures against the grain of their nature, but to render them free to follow their own deepest desire, which can lead them only to Himself. *For He has made them for Himself, and their hearts are restless until they find their rest in Him.*[7]

But now Hick is waffling, for it appears that we are not free after all. If so, Hick's position is inconsistent. To account for moral evil, Hick posits God's giving us incompatibilist freedom and genuine independence to choose for ourselves—even contrary to His desires for us. But given his affirmation of absolute creation and absolute foreknowledge, Hick sees that God's perfect goodness is possible only if not one soul is lost. To salvage God's goodness, Hick is forced to accept some mode of determinism that undermines his free-will defense. Hick's way out, as appealing as it first appears, seems on analysis to be incoherent.

Joseph Smith's Way Out

Joseph Smith's way out of the conceptual incoherency generated by the traditional theological premises is to not go in. His revelations circumvent the theoretical problem of evil by denying the trouble-making postulate of absolute creation—and, consequently, the classical definition of divine omnipotence. Contrary to classical Christian thought, Joseph explicitly affirmed that there are entities and structures which are co-eternal with God himself. On my reading of Joseph's discourse, these eternal entities include chaotic matter, intelligences (or what I will call primal persons), and lawlike structures or principles. According to Joseph Smith, God's creative activity consists of bringing order out of disorder, of organizing a cosmos out of chaos—not in the production of something out of nothing. Two statements from Joseph's King Follett sermon should give some sense of how radically his understanding of creation departs from the classical Christian notion. With respect to the Creation, Joseph wrote:

You ask the learned doctors why they say the world was made out of nothing; and they will answer, "Doesn't the Bible say He created the world?" And they infer, from the word create, that it must have been made out of nothing. Now, the word create came from the [Hebrew] word bau-rau which does not mean to create out of nothing; it means . . . to organize the world out of chaos—chaotic matter. . . . Element had an existence from the time [God] had. The pure principles of element are principles which can never be destroyed; they may be organized and reorganized, but not destroyed. They had no beginning, and can have no end.[8]

More particularly, with respect to the creation of man, Joseph added:

The mind of man—the immortal spirit. Where did it come from? All learned men and doctors of divinity say that God created it in the beginning; but it is not so. . . . I am going to tell of things more noble.

We say that God himself is a self-existent being. . . . [But] who told you that man did not exist in like manner upon the same principles? Man does exist upon the same principles. God made a tabernacle and put a spirit into it, and it became a living soul. . . . How does it read in the Hebrew? It does not say in the Hebrew that God created the spirit of man. It says, "God made man out of the earth and put into him Adam's spirit, and so became a living body."

The mind or the intelligence which man possesses is co-equal [co-eternal] with God himself."[9]

Elsewhere Joseph taught that there are also "laws of eternal and self-existent principles"[10]—normative structures of some kind, I take it, that constitute things as they (eternally) are. What are possible instances of such laws or principles? Lehi, I believe, made reference to some such principles in the enlightening (and comforting) explanation of evil he provided to his son Jacob as recorded in 2 Nephi 2 of the Book of Mormon. (I call that explanation Lehi's theodicy.) "Adam fell that men might be," Lehi told Jacob, "and men are, that they might have joy" (2 Nephi 2:25). But to attain this joy, Lehi explained that

it must needs be, that there is an opposition in all things. If not so . . . ,
righteousness could not be brought to pass, neither wickedness, neither
holiness nor misery, neither good nor bad. . . .

 And [so] *to bring about his eternal purposes in the end of man, after he*
had created our first parents . . . , it must needs be that there was an opposi-
tion; even the forbidden fruit in opposition to the tree of life; the one being
sweet and the other bitter.

 Wherefore, the Lord God gave unto man that he should act for him-
self. Wherefore, man could not act for himself save it should be that he was
enticed by the one or the other. [2 Nephi 2:11, 15–16]

According to Lehi, there are apparently states of affair that even
God, though omnipotent, cannot bring about. Man is that he might
have joy, but even God cannot bring about joy without moral righteousness, moral righteousness without moral freedom, or moral
freedom without an opposition in all things. With moral freedom as
an essential variable in the divine equation for man, two consequences
stand out saliently: (i) the inevitability of moral evil; and (ii) our need
for a Redeemer.

If my interpretation of 2 Nephi 2 is correct, then it seems as if
we ought to reject the classical definition of omnipotence in favor
of an understanding that fits better with the inspired text. Given
that text, how ought we understand divine omnipotence? B. H.
Roberts plausibly proposed that God's omnipotence be understood
as the power to bring about any state of affairs consistent with the
natures of eternal existences.[11] So understood, we can coherently
adopt an "instrumentalist" view of evil wherein pain, suffering, and
opposition become means of moral and spiritual development. God
is omnipotent, but He cannot prevent evil without preventing greater
goods or ends—the value of which more than offsets the dis-value of
the evil: soul-making, joy, eternal (or godlike) life.

Armed with Joseph Smith's doctrine of entities co-eternal with
God and our revised definition of divine omnipotence, let us consider
again the logical problem of evil and Flew's argument charging God
with complicity in all the world's evil. From Joseph Smith's theological

platform, it does not follow that God is the total or even the ultimate explanation of all else. Thus it is not an implication of Joseph's worldview that God is an accessory before the fact to all the world's evil. Nor does it follow that God is responsible for every moral and nonmoral defect that occurs in the world. Within a framework of eternal entities and structures that God did not create and that He cannot destroy, it seems to me that the logical problem of evil is dissolved. Evil is not logically inconsistent with the existence of God. Within the Prophet's worldview there can be saving explanations of the world's evil—explanations that in no way impugn God's loving-kindness. To see what such explanations might be like, we need to fill out the picture considerably. And to do so it will be useful to move from argument and analysis to narrative. Time does not allow me to do it, but I invite each of you, in reflecting on these matters, to rehearse again the old familiar and yet ever new and renewing story of the plan of salvation. To do so is to articulate a Mormon theodicy.

II. A SOTERIOLOGICAL PROBLEM OF EVIL

Earlier, when I first introduced the logical problem of evil, I argued that most discussions of the problem were too narrow and especially unfair to the Christian believer in that they failed to take into account the problem's strongest possible solution—the incarnation of God the Son in the person of Jesus of Nazareth and his triumph over sin, suffering, and death through His atonement and resurrection. But ironically, what I referred to as "the strongest possible solution" to the problem of evil when understood in traditional terms becomes, itself, part of the problem. How can this be?

This—the soteriological problem—arises out of the New Testament teaching that salvation comes through and *only* through Christ. For instance, John reports Jesus as having claimed this very thing: "I am the way, the truth, and the life: no man cometh unto the Father, but by me" (John 14:6). Similarly, Peter: "Neither is there salvation in any other: for there is none other name under heaven given among men, whereby we must be saved" (Acts 4:12).

Thomas Morris, professor of philosophy at Notre Dame, in his book *The Logic of God Incarnate*, puts the difficulty (which he calls a "scandal") this way:

The scandal . . . arises with a simple set of questions asked of the Christian theologian who claims that it is only through the life and death of God incarnated in Jesus Christ that all can be saved and reconciled to God: How can the many humans who lived and died before the time of Christ be saved through him? They surely cannot be held accountable for responding appropriately to something of which they could have no knowledge. Furthermore, what about all the people who have lived since the time of Christ in cultures with different religious traditions, untouched by the Christian gospel? How can they be excluded fairly from a salvation not ever really available to them? How could a just God set up a particular condition of salvation, the highest end of human life possible, which was and is inaccessible to most people? Is not the love of God better understood as universal, rather than as limited to a mediation through the one particular individual, Jesus of Nazareth? Is it not a moral as well as a religious scandal to claim otherwise?[12]

Claremont professor of philosophy Stephen Davis expresses a similar perplexity. In a recent issue of *Modern Theology* he put the problem this way:

Suppose there was a woman named Oohku who lived from 370–320 B.C. in the interior of Borneo. Obviously, she never heard of Jesus Christ or the Judeo-Christian God; she was never baptized, nor did she ever make any institutional or psychological commitment to Christ or to the Christian church. She couldn't have done these things; she was simply born in the wrong place and at the wrong time. Is it right for God to condemn this woman to eternal hell just because she was never able to come to God through Christ? Of course not. . . . God is just and loving.[13]

This problem that Morris and Davis state can be expressed in terms of an inconsistent triad, a set of three premises—all of which are apparently true, yet the conjunction of any two of which seemingly entails the denial of the third:

1. God is perfectly loving and just and desires that all of His children be saved.

2. Salvation comes only in and through one's acceptance of Christ.

3. Millions of God's children have lived and died without ever hearing of Christ or having a chance to receive salvation through Him.

Number 3 is indisputable, forcing us, it seems, to give up either 1 or 2—both of which seem clearly warranted on biblical authority. So how to resolve the puzzle? The issue is receiving much attention right now from keen and sensitive Christian thinkers. Proposed resolutions are many, ranging from "universalism" on one pole to "exclusivism" on the other. Universalists typically affirm premise 1, compelling them to deny the explicit New Testament teaching that salvation comes only in and through acceptance of Christ. Exclusivists usually affirm number 2, concluding that Oohku, and millions of others like her, must be lost. But this leaves *them* at a loss to square their view with number 1. Neither view is satisfactory.

Many of you in the audience are, no doubt, smiling, recognizing that adding a premise 4 to the triad resolves the puzzle:

4. Those who live and die without having a chance to respond positively to the gospel of Jesus Christ will have that chance postmortemly.

Thank God for Joseph Smith! And not merely for resolving one more thorny problem of evil—which he surely did (or, God did, through him)—but for being the instrument through whom God restored the knowledge and priesthood powers that make the redemption of the dead possible. Elder John Taylor wrote truly when he penned these words: "Joseph Smith, the Prophet and Seer of the Lord, has done more, save Jesus only, for the salvation of men in this world, than any other man that ever lived in it" (D&C 135:3).

III. THE PRACTICAL PROBLEM OF EVIL

I want to finish by considering the Prophet Joseph Smith's contribution to the practical problem of evil—the challenge of living trustingly and faithfully in the face of what personally seems to be overwhelming evil. Joseph left us much by way of revelation that speaks to *this* problem of evil, but perhaps his own life speaks more powerfully than the words.

Joseph was no stranger to sorrow. He spoke, though inspired by God, from the crucible of his own experience. In D&C 127:2, the Prophet reflected: "The envy and wrath of man have been my common lot all the days of my life. . . . Deep water is what I am wont to swim in." Indeed, Joseph faced continual persecution. He was tarred and feathered, subjected to numerous lawsuits, and confined in intolerable conditions in dungeon-like jails. He was deeply affected by the deaths of his brothers Alvin and Don Carlos, and his father also died prematurely. Four of his 11 children, including twin sons, died at childbirth, and a fifth died at 14 months. Joseph was never financially well-to-do and was often impoverished. For much of his life he had no regular place to call home. After the failure of the bank in Kirtland, many of his friends turned against him. Members of the Church published the *Nauvoo Expositor* for the purposes of denouncing him, and this event eventually culminated in his martyrdom. Even Joseph, who walked so closely with God, on occasion in his life experienced the troubling sense of God's absence when he felt God should have been there for him.

A case in point: the dark days of 1838 when the Saints were driven from Missouri. The setting was as follows: A vast number of Mormon families had been burned out of their homes by mobs. Fathers were tied to trees and bullwhipped. Thirty-four people, including men and children, had been massacred at a settlement known as Haun's Mill. Shortly thereafter, the Mormon settlement at Far West, Missouri, was besieged and sacked by the state militia. Soldiers raped some of the women so many times that they died from the torture. Joseph Smith had been betrayed by a friend and turned over to military mobsters to be killed. He was taken to a small dungeon called Liberty Jail. During the four months of imprisonment, Joseph and his companions were abused, fed human flesh, and left in filthy conditions.

Joseph Smith felt abandoned by God. In a prayer Joseph questioned from the depths of his soul:

> *O God, where art thou? And where is the pavilion that covereth thy hiding place?*
>
> *How long shall thy hand be stayed, and thine eye, yea thy pure eye, behold from the eternal heavens the wrongs of thy people?* [D&C 121:1–2]

In response to this prayer of the soul's desperation, Joseph heard God:

> *My son, peace be unto thy soul; thine adversity and thine afflictions shall be but a small moment;*
>
> *And then, if thou endure it well, God shall exalt thee on high. . . .*
>
> *. . . Know thou, my son, that all these things shall give thee experience, and shall be for thy good.*
>
> *The Son of Man hath descended below them all. Art thou greater than he?* [D&C 121:7–8; 122:7–8]

Confronted with what seemed to be overwhelming evil, Joseph found meaning in his suffering, maintained hope, trusted God, and kept the faith. And God spoke peace.

CONCLUSION

As I have perused the philosophical literature on the problem of evil, noted men's perplexities, and then returned to once more ponder the revelations and teachings of Joseph Smith, I have been constantly amazed. Joseph had no training in theology, no doctor of divinity degree; his formal education was at best scanty. And yet through him comes light that dissolves the profoundest paradoxes and strengthens and edifies me through my own personal trials. The world calls him "an enigma," but I know that the inspiration of the Almighty gave him understanding. I bear witness that he was a prophet of God. In the sacred name of Jesus Christ, amen.

NOTES

1. At the outset, I must acknowledge my debt to others for much that appears in this address. My thinking on the subject was first stimulated by reading many years ago Truman Madsen's *Eternal Man*—a classic that ought to be reprinted. My thinking has been further shaped by conversations and collaborative work with Blake Ostler. Indeed, some of my text today is taken from that work. Finally, my thinking has been refined by numerous in-class and out-of-class discussions with hundreds of students over the past 27 years. To these students and to Truman and Blake, I express gratitude.

2. David Hume, *Dialogues Concerning Natural Religion*, ed. Nelson Pike (Indianapolis: Bobbs-Merrill, 1970), 91.

3. Anthony Flew, section D of "Theology and Falsification," chapter 6 in Antony Flew and Alasdair MacIntyre, eds., *New Essays in Philosophical Theology* (New York: Macmillan, 1955), 107.

4. John Hick, *Evil and the God of Love* (New York: Harper and Row, 1966), 326.

5. Ibid., 376.

6. C. S. Lewis, chapter 8, "Hell," *The Problem of Pain* (New York: Macmillan, 1962), 127; emphasis in original.

7. Hick, *Evil*, 380–81; emphasis added.

8. Joseph Smith, *Teachings of the Prophet Joseph Smith*, sel. Joseph Fielding Smith (Salt Lake City: Deseret Book Company, 1976), 350–52; emphasis in original.

9. Ibid., 352–53.

10. Ibid., 181.

11. See B. H. Roberts, *The Seventy's Course in Theology*, vol. 2 (Dallas, Texas: S. K. Taylor Publishing Company, 1976), fourth year, lesson 12, 70.

12. Thomas V. Morris, *The Logic of God Incarnate* (Ithaca, New York: Cornell University Press, 1986), 174–75.

13. Stephen T. Davis, "Universalism, Hell, and the Fate of the Ignorant," in *Modern Theology* 6, no. 2 (January 1990): 176; emphasis in original.

But for Joseph

Katherine D. Pullins

I have entitled my discussion with you today "But for Joseph," which is appropriate since on this day, the 27th of June, we commemorate each year the end of the Prophet Joseph Smith's earthly mission. However, let me preface my remarks with a little background information.

First, I must say that I'll never again complain about being given an assigned topic for a talk. Any restrictiveness is far outweighed by the overwhelming feeling of having the entire universe of gospel subjects laid out before you. When I heard the date of this devotional, I knew that the Prophet Joseph would be a part of what I would address today, most likely as an excellent illustration of qualities we should cultivate in our lives. However, since I am not a Church historian, I didn't plan to have Joseph be *the* topic. But I am a convert to the religion Joseph Smith restored, and today I will be speaking unabashedly about that conversion. If you are not a Latter-day Saint, I invite you to listen with an open mind and heart.

Katherine D. Pullins was associate dean of the J. Reuben Clark Law School at BYU when this devotional talk was given on 27 June 2000. © Brigham Young University.

It is that firsthand journey from the Prophet being an example to the entire focus of this talk that I will try to describe to you today. As I researched and read, interviewed and soul searched, my testimony of the Prophet Joseph moved from the factual to the very personal. So instead of discussing in a general way "But for Joseph, how different would the world be?" I have asked myself and I am asking you to consider now, "But for Joseph, how different would *my life* be?"

I first heard the name Joseph Smith during the summer after my sophomore year in high school. I had attended a conference with a group of teenage girls, and we were returning from Galveston to our homes in El Paso, Texas. It was a long bus ride, and I think more to preserve our chaperones' sanity than to give us an educational experience, we stopped in San Antonio, where the HemisFair, an event akin to the world's fair, was being held. The adults turned us loose for several hours to visit the various pavilions, and my group of six soon found its way to one entitled "Man's Search for Happiness." When we discovered we had accidentally stumbled into a religious presentation, we tried to exit the side door—but those clever missionaries had locked it! We were stuck, so we feigned attention until the audience moved into the next room and we could escape through some unlocked doors. When we boarded the bus later that afternoon for what was still a long ride home, I noticed that the only piece of reading material I had managed to hold onto—not coincidentally, I believe now—during our dash through the fair was a pamphlet with Joseph Smith's picture on the front. I read through it, motivated only by a need to pass the time, and mentally categorized it as "curious."

The following spring, in my American history class, I was searching for an engaging topic for a term paper. It was a time when newspaper headlines spoke of civil rights and of legally atoning for past injustices. I would have preferred to do a paper on current events and discrimination against groups the majority labeled as "different," but it was a history class. As I looked at a time line of the 1800s in one of the reference books, the persecutions against the Mormons captured my attention. I chose to take an objective (which turned out to be far more sympathetic) look back at the events that forced this peculiar religious group westward. The name Joseph Smith turned up again as I researched the topic in history books and encyclopedias.

Over the years when someone has asked about my conversion, I have not typically included these previous two experiences. My story usually began with the events that immediately preceded my hearing the missionary lessons. I think I had discounted these two experiences because of my resistance to the message in the first instance and my factual, even sterile, approach in the second. I feel differently today. I am convinced that these incidents provided background for my later acceptance of the gospel. They were an introduction to the concept of a recent prophet and a factual placement of events in time. Without this context I feel I would not have been sufficiently primed to accept, relatively quickly, the missionaries' message about what God revealed to a 14-year-old boy in the spring of 1820. I believe these were preparatory steps, and the Lord, knowing me, was customizing my instruction.

For about two years prior to that evening when I sat in my living room and listened to the missionaries present the first discussion, I had been on a "spiritual quest." I had grown up in a family that valued Christian ideals such as honesty, fair treatment of others, and kindness, but I did not have a spiritual dimension in my life, and I longed for one. I felt a growing need, an urgency, really, to fix my mind and heart on the divine, so I began to study about and visit different churches. I approached each new introduction to the members of a congregation and the denomination's beliefs and doctrine optimistically. I didn't understand it completely at the time, but I had a two-part screening system in place: First I would try to take a spiritual reading, a check of how I was feeling, early in the visit; then I would turn to the doctrinal aspects and ask questions about the true purpose of life, the hereafter, and how these affected the way one lived now. None of the churches I visited passed even the first part of my test, and I was getting discouraged.

Now back to that evening in 1970: After a brief discussion of the Apostasy, the missionaries reverently explained the Restoration brought about through the Prophet Joseph Smith. They presented in some detail that curious story I had quickly read about in the pamphlet two years earlier. I felt my initial optimism that this church could be my spiritual destination slip away, and doubts crowded into my mind. Did they actually believe that God had appeared to someone just last century? And to a boy younger than I was rather than to a wise, aged prophet? While I formed my questions, the missionaries moved on to a flannel-board presentation with circles and lines that depicted the plan of salvation. Before long I felt that their explanation was somehow familiar to me, and they had my full attention. I was certain that they were speaking the truth in this part of their presentation, and I felt some hope return. As the missionaries were leaving, they scheduled our next appointment, handed me a copy of *The Joseph Smith Story*, and asked me to commit to read it carefully and pray about it. I agreed to do so.

Later that night, my roller coaster of emotions hit a low point. As I thought back on all I had heard and felt during the evening and weighed the positives and negatives in my mind, I believed that I would cancel the next appointment I had set. But first I decided to keep my promise to the missionaries. After I had read the Prophet's narrative of the First Vision and beyond, I offered up an awkward, short prayer. Sleep came quickly, so I was not left to ponder the message for long. The next morning, as I knelt again in prayer, I found that the Spirit had eased my doubts about Joseph Smith's account and confirmed the truths of which he testified. I kept the appointment with the sister missionaries, and that decision has made all the difference in my life. But for Joseph, I would not have found my spiritual home in the restored gospel of Jesus Christ.

At the time, that level of understanding and testimony was sufficient for me to go forth with my study, baptism, and confirmation. When the Lord told the members of his newly formed church, "For his word ye shall receive, as if from mine own mouth, in all patience and faith" (D&C 21:5), He most likely was admonishing some whose faith was at such an early stage as mine was then. Patience and faith are essential elements in the development of our testimonies, but our progression must be accelerated in these latter days. After visiting the Sacred Grove on one occasion, President Gordon B. Hinckley wrote in his journal that he felt an "ever-growing compulsion to bear testimony of the divinity of the Lord and of the mission of the Prophet Joseph Smith. I think this world needs this more than any other thing" (in Sheri Dew, *Go Forward with Faith* [Salt Lake City: Deseret Book Company, 1996], 326).

Preparing this talk has forced me to assess the testimony I began to build 30 years ago of the Prophet Joseph and the eternal truths he restored. I know that this initial and essential conviction has been strengthened by study, prayer, and life's experience; but I needed to draw closer, to look deeper at his mission. The Prophet Joseph served as a divine conduit in bringing to light marvelous and precious truths. In his eyewitness account of the Martyrdom, President John Taylor summed up Joseph's contribution:

> *Joseph Smith, the Prophet and Seer of the Lord, has done more, save Jesus only, for the salvation of men in this world, than any other man that ever lived in it. . . .* [He has] *left a fame and name that cannot be slain. He lived great, and he died great in the eyes of God and his people; and like most of the Lord's anointed in ancient times, has sealed his mission and his works with his own blood.* [D&C 135:3]

In a space of approximately 24 years, the Prophet Joseph accomplished much that has eternal, historical, and personal implications for each of us. As I attempt to list the following four of his contributions and the ways each has particular meaning in my life, I encourage you to make your own list.

1. Joseph Smith opened up communication with the heavens.
Because he was willing to ask God directly, the Prophet Joseph—and each of us through him—learned eternal truths about the nature of God and the current status of God's kingdom on earth. He learned that the forces of the adversary are real and combat all that is righteous and pure. Joseph also learned that the Father and the resurrected Lord are separate beings who knew him and spoke to him by way of instruction. He learned that none of the churches on the earth

at that time had the truth and that he should join none of them. In his book *Here We Stand,* Joseph Fielding McConkie underscored the personal implications the First Vision holds for each of us:

> *The way we answer questions about our faith ought to be by finding the quickest and most direct route to the Sacred Grove. That is our ground. It is sacred ground. It is where the heavens are opened and the God of heaven speaks. It is where testimonies are born and the greatest truths of heaven are unveiled.* [*Here We Stand* (Salt Lake City: Deseret Book Company, 1995), 6]

But for the Prophet Joseph's experience in the Sacred Grove, I would not have an understanding of the loving nature of God and my literal claim to divine heritage, described in Doctrine and Covenants 25:1: "All those who receive my gospel are sons and daughters in my kingdom." The God I had learned about before I accepted the gospel was removed, ever-judging, and powerful. However, I had an experience as a young child that was not consistent with this unapproachable image of deity. At that time I was living in rural Arkansas. Because I had no brothers or sisters, I had adopted an agreeable farm dog as my constant companion. One afternoon as we were walking home along a single-lane road, she was struck and killed by a truck as I looked on. That night, as I tried to fall asleep, my grief overwhelmed me. Before long that grief turned into fear that I, too, might die suddenly. No one was near enough in the house to console me, so I offered up a prayer, and my pleading was heard. I felt encircled by warm, loving arms and instinctively knew I was being comforted by my Father. As the missionaries explained the nature of a loving Heavenly Father who answered young Joseph Smith's prayer, my experience 13 years earlier came immediately to my mind and validated their words.

2. Joseph Smith translated ancient scripture and recorded modern-day revelation.

With the assistance of his scribes, Joseph's unceasing efforts resulted in the translation of the Book of Mormon, another testament of Jesus Christ; the Pearl of Great Price; and the publication of the Doctrine and Covenants. Can you imagine your life without the precepts, the images, and the understanding that the Book of Mormon lends? We know that "the Book of Mormon [is] the most correct of any book on earth, and the keystone of our religion, and a man [can] get nearer to God by abiding by its precepts, than by any other book" (*HC* 4:461). But for Joseph, we would not have this book of scripture. Think how limited our understanding would be if we did not have Father Lehi's vision of the tree of life. What a loss if we did not have the opportunity to know Nephi, Alma, Moroni, and others through their own words. How incomplete our view of the Savior's ministry would be if we did not have at our fingertips the tender account in 3 Nephi of Him with His "other sheep" in America. And how lacking our understanding of the creation would be without the accounts recorded in the books of Moses and Abraham. Without the intensive instruction in Church history and covenant-making and -keeping in the Doctrine and Covenants, would we be able to truly appreciate the legacy of our faith's past and be prepared to serve in the kingdom?

3. Through his persistent and resilient efforts, Joseph Smith brought people to their Savior Jesus Christ.

In this dispensation the Prophet Joseph literally brought heaven closer to earth as he lifted the darkness of apostasy, banished it, and brought to light the Savior's plain and precious doctrine. He was the chosen instrument of the Lord who was called both to distinguish the true, restored church from other denominations and to bring forth the power and purity of Christ's true doctrines. Joseph F. Smith stated in *Gospel Doctrine*:

> *I believe in the divinity of Jesus Christ, because more than ever I come nearer the possession of the actual knowledge that Jesus is the Christ, the Son of the living God, through the testimony of Joseph Smith . . . that he today stands before the world as the last great, actual, living, witness of the divinity of Christ's mission and His power to redeem man from the temporal death and also from the second death. . . . Thank God for Joseph Smith.*
> [*GD*, 495]

Thus the Prophet Joseph provided the needed linkage to the Savior who, as the Great Mediator, connects us to the Father (see D&C 76:22–24). Indeed, Joseph taught that

the fundamental principles of our religion are the testimony of the Apostles and Prophets, concerning Jesus Christ, that He died, was buried, and rose again the third day, and ascended into heaven; and all other things which pertain to our religion are only appendages to it. [*Teachings,* 121]

But for Joseph, my understanding of the Atonement still would be theoretical and abstract. I would not have the information that tells me that the Savior's sacrifice was, yes, infinite and all-encompassing, but also very specifically *for me.* Understanding the personal nature and application of the Atonement allows me to know that, after all I can do, my Savior and Redeemer in His mercy can complete my circle of repentance and growth and lift my soul. He can and has changed my heart when no amount of study, willpower, or well-intended advice could affect my need. I am thankful to know that this greatest of gifts can make me, in spite of my weaknesses, more fit for His service.

4. Joseph Smith established the kingdom of God on earth today.

Under divine tutelage, the Prophet Joseph organized the Church. He directed the construction of the Kirtland and Nauvoo Temples and restored the ordinances of the house of the Lord for the benefit of individuals and families. He was ordained to the holy priesthood, and, through him, its powers and blessings were restored to the earth. Joseph saw that missionaries were sent forth to take the gospel not only to surrounding areas but also to Europe and the isles of the sea. He established the Relief Society for the sisters that they might have opportunities to extend charity to those in need and to save souls.

But for Joseph, I could not be a participant in the building of the kingdom of God today. Without the fellowship of my brothers and sisters in the gospel, I would not be strengthened and sustained. Since my baptism I have had only a few times when I was unable to associate with the Saints, and then it was for only a short period of time.

But how I missed their kind counsel and that communication from spirit to spirit.

I can't imagine my life without the refuge and perspective of the temple. If the sacred ordinances that are performed therein were not on the earth today, I would not have the understanding of eternal marriage that stands firm in the face of trials and challenges. I am so grateful that our son, Brandt, and his wife, Lori, currently have the privilege of serving in the Washington D.C. Temple. Brandt recently wrote in an e-mail:

> *Last night was our night to work in the temple, and while I was officiating, I heard myself speaking the incredible blessings that are promised, and was overwhelmed by the great mercy and love that our Father shows us by extending those blessings to us and giving me the opportunity to help pronounce those blessings upon others who are anxiously waiting for them on both sides of the veil.*
>
> *What a wonderful blessing it is to live when the fullness of the gospel, the fullness of the priesthood, and the fullness of the blessings of our Savior's Atonement are here and waiting for all!*

I, too, marvel at the blessings that are ours because temples are now among us. In a little over a month, our son Micah will be sealed for time and all eternity to a beautiful daughter of God in the Lord's house. All of our sons, the two daughters they have added to our family, and other loved ones will witness that all-important moment in eternity. Today my heart nearly bursts with gratitude just thinking about the occasion. But for Joseph, those priesthood keys could not be exercised in our behalf.

And without the priesthood, and a husband worthy and willing to call down blessings of comfort, healing, and strength upon our family, the world's "three Ds"—distraction, discouragement, and despair— would never be far away from our door. And without the selfless sacrifice of missionary work, I literally would not be with you today. In addition, my husband and sons would never have had the privilege of seeking out and bringing into the fold people who at first appeared so different in language and custom but soon became quite literally their brothers and sisters.

Recently our oldest son Travis traveled to Florida to be at Miami International Airport when Elder Franklyn Tavarez returned from his mission in Michigan. When he was serving in the Fort Lauderdale Mission, Travis had the privilege of baptizing Frankie when he was a young teenager. How I wish I could have witnessed the embrace that they shared as brothers and fellow missionaries upon his arrival!

Our missionary son, Taylor, who is completing his mission in Chile next month, recently shared his testimony with us in a letter:

> *I know this work is true. I know that the standard of truth has been erected. I feel the power of the priesthood when I humbly use it. I know that Jesus is our Savior. I will forever be grateful for the gospel in my life and will forever defend the truth and this, the Lord's Church.*

Having the privilege to serve full-time and never-ending missions that bring souls unto Christ through the gospel that Joseph restored is the sweetest work to which we can devote ourselves.

But for Joseph, the Relief Society would not have been divinely organized. I love this organization and the privilege it affords me to serve with the exceptional sisters of the Church. That is another talk for another day, but let me just say that when Joseph told his beloved Emma and the sisters gathered in 1842 that he "turn[ed] the key" in their behalf, under the direction of the priesthood of God, Heavenly Father provided a structure for his daughters to have firsthand experience with both extending and receiving Christlike service (see page 32 of "Minutes of the Nauvoo Female Relief Society," 28 April 1842, LDS Church Historical Department, Salt Lake City).

Thus we are all eternally indebted to the Prophet Joseph Smith. How do we demonstrate that gratitude? Let me suggest three ways.

1. We can seek to love and honor the Prophet Joseph as we learn more of his life and his mission.

After spending this time researching the Prophet, I realized that I did not know enough about him as an individual. The first quality that comes to my mind now when I think of him is humility. From his earnest plea in the Sacred Grove to his nobility in Liberty Jail and at Carthage, Joseph set aside all pride and sublimated his will to the Father and His work. In his book *Mere Christianity*, C. S. Lewis described a humble man not as someone with downcast eyes who is always underrepresenting his worth and contribution. Rather, he said, if you were to meet a humble man,

probably all you will think about him is that he seemed a cheerful, intelligent chap who took a real interest in what you *said to* him. *If you do dislike him it will be because you feel a little envious of anyone who seems to enjoy life so easily. He will not be thinking about humility: he will not be thinking about himself at all.* [*Mere Christianity* (New York: Macmillan, 1952), 114; book 3, chapter 8, paragraph 13; emphasis in original]

This was the Prophet Joseph.

And the Prophet did enjoy life. President Joseph F. Smith described Joseph:

O, he was full of joy; he was full of gladness; he was full of love. . . . And while he could play with children and amuse himself at simple, innocent games among men, he also communed with the Father and the Son and spoke with angels, and they visited him, and conferred blessings and gifts and keys of power upon him. [Joseph F. Smith, in Brian H. Stuy, comp., *Collected Discourses*, 5 vols. (Burbank, California: B.H.S. Publishing, 1987–92), 5:29]

Wouldn't it have been wonderful to spend time with this man, this prophet? I believe that we would each have loved him in a very personal way. President Brigham Young expressed his feelings for Joseph with great enthusiasm:

I feel like shouting hallelujah, all the time, when I think that I ever knew Joseph Smith, the Prophet whom the Lord raised up and ordained, and to whom He gave keys and power to build up the kingdom of God on earth and sustain it. [*JD* 3:51]

The Prophet inspired love in those who knew him best. The Prophet's nephew, President Joseph F. Smith, also stated, "Where [Joseph Smith's name] is spoken of for good, . . . they revere him, and they love him, as they love no other man" (*GD*, 481). At the dedication of the Joseph Smith Memorial Building, President Gordon B. Hinckley summed up his feelings for the Prophet by simply exclaiming , "I love the Prophet Joseph Smith. I love the Prophet Joseph Smith!" (in "A Heroic Figure," *Ensign*, September 1990, 38). Brothers and sisters, I can now join these brethren and say I love this man, this prophet.

2. We can bear testimony of Joseph Smith's crucial role in this dispensation.

The Prophet reminded all members of the Church, "When you joined this Church you enlisted to serve God. When you did that you left the neutral ground, and you never can get back on to it" (Daniel Tyler, in "Recollections of the Prophet Joseph Smith," *Juvenile Instructor* 27, no. 16 [15 August 1892]: 492). Our testimonies cannot be generic; they cannot be neutral on the subject of the life and mission of the Prophet. We are instructed in Doctrine and Covenants 31:4, "You shall declare the things which have been revealed to my servant, Joseph Smith." And we should never testify of revelations without acknowledging the revelator. Brigham Young's logic on this point was direct and profound:

If Jesus lives, and is the Saviour of the world, Joseph Smith is a Prophet of God, and lives in the bosom of his father Abraham. Though they have killed his body, yet he lives and beholds the face of his Father in heaven; and his garments are pure as the angels that surround the throne of God; and no man on the earth can say that Jesus lives, and deny at the same time my assertion about the Prophet Joseph. [*JD* 1:38]

In section 122 of the Doctrine and Covenants, the Lord told Joseph:

The ends of the earth shall inquire after thy name, and fools shall have thee in derision, and hell shall rage against thee;

While the pure in heart, and the wise, and the noble, and the virtuous, shall seek counsel, and authority, and blessings constantly from under thy hand. [D&C 122:1–2]

And in section 6 the Lord admonished us, "Therefore be diligent; stand by my servant Joseph, faithfully, in whatsoever difficult circumstances he may be for the word's sake" (D&C 6:18). May we demonstrate by the testimonies we bear that we are diligently standing by him and can be counted among those who revere Joseph's name and essential role.

3. We can serve continuously and faithfully in building the kingdom.

In the *Lectures on Faith*, Joseph charged us to live as he had:

Let us here observe, that a religion that does not require the sacrifice of all things never has power sufficient to produce the faith necessary unto life and salvation; for, from the first existence of man, the faith necessary unto the enjoyment of life and salvation never could be obtained without the sacrifice of all earthly things. [*Lectures on Faith* 6:7]

In the Church we experience different seasons of service. In each calling we have the opportunity to sacrifice more of ourselves than we ever have before. We honor Joseph by serving well, literally consecrating our efforts in doing that which no one else can accomplish at that time and in that place to serve the Master.

As I close today, I want to thank those two sister missionaries and their stake counterparts who, 30 years ago, challenged me to read and pray about the Prophet Joseph's story. I also am immensely grateful to those who, in recent months, have helped me know Joseph better as a man and a foreordained prophet. My family and friends have expressed unwavering support and encouragement. At a moment of despair when a significant part of my text for this talk had somehow "evaporated" into cyberspace, Heidi Swinton, who wrote last year's amazing PBS production *An American Prophet*, took time she didn't have to lend me perspective. I also appreciate Liz Lemon Swindle, the gifted artist, who has brought Joseph closer to our hearts through her paintings and has allowed me to share some of them with you today.

On this occasion we are gathered here as Saints in a building that bears the Prophet's name because of what happened in that Sacred Grove. And on this anniversary of the Martyrdom, I join with President Hinckley in reminding us that the accomplishments of the life of the Prophet Joseph Smith will never be blurred. The testimony of Joseph lives on.

Now, my brothers and sisters, most of you will not be asked to make such sacrifices or to respond to such calls. But what you do with your lives as you live them from day to day is no less important. ["Let Us Move This Work Forward," *Ensign*, November 1985, 85]

Whatever our present calling or opportunity, may we carry on his work. By so doing, we honor Joseph's memory and bring glory to our Savior and our Father.

Brothers and sisters, I challenge all of us, at whatever level—even if we are at a very early stage in our journey of faith—to deepen our understanding of the Prophet Joseph and his divine mission, to acknowledge before our Father and all who will listen that, but for the Prophet's role in this dispensation, our lives would be barren and our hope would fail us. I speak from personal experience when I say to you that seeking this new level of testimony will not come easily; the adversary will attempt to block your progress. It will require a letting go of pride and the things of this world that confuse and distract you. You will need to make a higher level of commitment to the work that the Prophet Joseph died to further. But all the effort is worth it, and it is essential that you commit yourself to it. For me, the strengthening of my testimony of the Prophet Joseph seemed to come together in a single moment. All of the historical and spiritual pieces fell into place as I read the simple, direct statement of the Lord to his beloved servant Joseph—and to each of us—in Doctrine and Covenants 5:10: "But this generation shall have my word through you."

I have glimpsed his earnest desire, unstoppable faith, the discouragement he made productive, and his feelings of enveloping joy, and I can now testify, with a conviction born of love for the Prophet Joseph and inexpressible gratitude for his mission, that he is a prophet of God. I say this in the name of Jesus Christ, amen.

"Stand by My Servant Joseph"

Cecil O. Samuelson

I am grateful, with Sister Samuelson, to be with you as we begin a new year and a new semester. I hope you share my enthusiasm for our opportunities and prospects in 2005. I also hope you have not yet broken all of your New Year's resolutions!

As you know, the year 2005 is the bicentennial anniversary of the birth of the Prophet Joseph Smith. During this year, throughout the Church and here at BYU, we will hear much and be reminded frequently of the life and mission of our Prophet of the Restoration. I am grateful to be able to add my voice to the millions of others who will honor this great man in so many ways in the days ahead.

Just last November we were privileged to hear from Sister Heidi Swinton, who spoke at our campus devotional on the topic "Joseph Smith: Lover of the Cause of Christ." It was a masterful address that presented history, facts, truth, and testimony. Now that our devotional presentations are so readily available, I'll not take time to repeat much of what she said. I do want to draw attention to one of

Cecil O. Samuelson was BYU president when this devotional address was delivered on 18 January 2005. © *Intellectual Reserve, Inc.*

those lines or phrases that has caused me to reflect, assess, think, and recommit myself. It is one that evokes sweet memories and striking insights.

Sister Swinton mentioned a verse from section 6 of the Doctrine and Covenants that was given to Oliver Cowdery during the time he served as Joseph's scribe while he was translating the Book of Mormon. She also reminded us that this instruction was not just for Oliver but is for all of us as well (see D&C 25:16). This is what the Lord said: "Therefore be diligent; stand by my servant Joseph, faithfully, in whatsoever difficult circumstances he may be for the word's sake" (D&C 6:18).

The phrase "stand by my servant Joseph" is the one that especially caught my attention. What did it mean to Oliver, and what should it mean to us?

The word *stand* has many meanings. The footnote in our scriptures suggests two words as possible synonyms for our special consideration. They are *diligence* and *loyalty.* I believe there are other definitions or constructions that might also apply. I intend to consider some of them with you.

Before I do, let me mention some of the things we know very well about the Prophet Joseph. From the very beginning, even before the Church was organized, it became clear that Joseph Smith was no ordinary young man. Although born into modest means and circumstances, he quickly was identified as someone very special. You are aware of his early experiences. The First Vision was an unexpected occurrence that not only changed his life forever but literally changed the history of the world. His initial interview with the angel Moroni, occurring while he was just 17 years old, taught him that his life and work would not be usual by any measure.

Listen to these words from his history:

He called me by name, and said unto me that he was a messenger sent from the presence of God to me, and that his name was Moroni; that God had a work for me to do; and that my name should be had for good and evil among all nations, kindreds, and tongues, or that it should be both good and evil spoken of among all people. [JS—H 1:33]

That is an amazing prophecy for any 17-year-old. Think of the statistical improbability of the assertion that his "name should be had for good and evil" so broadly around the world. Yet the name of Joseph Smith is widely known among virtually all of the nations of the earth.

Of those who have heard of Joseph, their knowledge and understanding are highly variable and usually incomplete in very important ways. The Church and its leaders, missionaries, and other representatives are doing, and will do, much to improve what the world knows and understands of Joseph Smith. All of us will have parts to play, and our roles will be important.

The understanding that people have of him occurs at different levels. Let me mention a few. I hope as I mention these that you might mentally note where you stand and which level best describes you.

Recognition: Increasingly, people recognize the name Joseph Smith and are able to relate him to The Church of Jesus Christ of Latter-day Saints, the Book of Mormon, and other basics of our faith. Some know enough, or believe that they know enough, to have developed opinions about him—positive or negative. Probably most people throughout the world fit into this category and are not exercised about him sufficiently to try and learn more. It is important that this group should not include any of us.

Appreciation: Of those who recognize the Prophet Joseph by name, there are those who know that he accomplished some things that have made a difference. They know that he organized a church and movement that has grown dramatically and has influenced many lives. Although they may or may not believe in his work or admire his contributions, they acknowledge that the world is different because of his life and efforts.

Admiration: Many who appreciate that Joseph made a difference also admire many of his accomplishments and contributions.

Although still not necessarily subscribing to his teachings or his mission, they admire what he did in Kirtland, Missouri, and Nauvoo. They admire his ability to enlist a following and to inspire people to sacrifice greatly for the cause he espoused. Again, not all who admire his accomplishments necessarily endorse his positions, even when they speak with admiration of some of the fruits of the gospel as he taught it.

Testimony: A subset of those who recognize, appreciate, and admire the Prophet Joseph are those who have a testimony of the truthfulness of his mission, his teachings, and his accounts of encounters with heavenly beings. They have no reservations about him or the doctrines he revealed, but they may not have fully internalized what this should mean to them.

True loyalty (or those who stand by him): Some, and I hope this includes you, have a testimony of the Prophet Joseph Smith and his unique and special mission. It is to you that I frame my question: What does it mean to "stand by my servant Joseph"? It means more than just recognition, appreciation—even admiration, belief, and testimony. The counsel given to Oliver Cowdery is illustrative of what I mean. To Oliver's great credit, he never denied his testimony of the events and experiences he had with Joseph Smith. Unfortunately, he did not live up to what the Lord required of him and lost his place to one more faithful (see D&C 124:95).

Another who was trusted and given great privileges and responsibility—as well as being instructed to stand by Joseph—was John C. Bennett (see D&C 124:16). Unfortunately, he not only was disloyal to Joseph, he lost his testimony as well, which is not uncommon with those who transgress (see D&C 68:16).

As you know, the one called to replace Oliver and enjoy the privileges, responsibilities, and destiny with the Prophet Joseph was his brother Hyrum. Without contrasting Hyrum with others unnecessarily, let us examine how Hyrum responded to his charge to stand by Joseph. There are many examples. Let me focus on just one for now (see D&C 11).

Even before the Church was organized, Hyrum, Joseph's older brother by five years, knew the truthfulness of what Joseph was teaching and reporting. He wanted to do his part and hoped and pled to be called as a missionary. I believe that you will want to study carefully the entire 11th section of the Doctrine and Covenants, which is the answer given by the Lord through Joseph Smith to Hyrum's entreaty. A useful exercise is to count the number of times in these verses that Hyrum is told that his work is to "keep the commandments." Let me just repeat part of the oft-quoted verse that must have been both a test and a trial for Hyrum.

"Seek not to declare my word, but first seek to obtain my word" (D&C 11:21). I suppose, had Hyrum been inclined, that he could have been just as offended as were Oliver and others when Joseph, acting in his role as president and prophet, had to tell them the hard truth as well. To Hyrum's everlasting credit, in spite of his initial disappointment that he was not to be a missionary at that time, he stood by Joseph and received the blessings God reserves for those most loyal and trusted. These blessings included, less than a year later, the exact opportunity that Hyrum had initially sought (see D&C 23:3).

Another who stood by Joseph was Brigham Young. Think of his loyalty. He said, "I feel like shouting hallejujah [*sic*], all the time, when I think that I ever knew Joseph Smith" (*JD* 3:51). We don't have time today to catalog all of the times Brigham demonstrated his complete fealty to Joseph, but the Prophet recognized and appreciated it. Near the end of his life Joseph said, "Of the [original] Twelve Apostles chosen in Kirtland, . . . there have been but two but what have lifted their heel against me—namely Brigham Young and Heber C. Kimball" (*HC* 5:412).

Grateful are we that there were others besides Hyrum, Brigham, and Heber C. Kimball who stood by Joseph even when it may have seemed to many to be folly to do so. Interestingly, but not surprisingly, it was from this group who stood by Joseph that replacements for the Twelve and other key leadership responsibilities were later selected. Let me mention just two of them.

John Taylor, who would follow Brigham Young as Joseph's successor, was converted to the Restoration by an apostle who later wavered for a period before returning to stand by Joseph. John Taylor, however, was stalwart from the time of his baptism in 1836. During the dark days in Kirtland he attended a meeting where President Joseph Smith, not in attendance, was severely criticized by apostates who once had been Joseph's friends and associates. John Taylor courageously offered this defense:

It was Joseph Smith, under the Almighty, who developed the first principles, and to him we must look for further instructions. If the spirit which he manifests does not bring blessings, I am very much afraid that the one manifested by those who have spoken, will not be very likely to secure them. The children of Israel, formerly, after seeing the power of God manifested in their midst, fell into rebellion and idolatry, and there is certainly very great danger of us doing the same thing. [In B. H. Roberts, *The Life of John Taylor* (Salt Lake City: Bookcraft, 1963), 41]

John Taylor saw what had happened to his colleagues and recognized the attendant spiritual risks that they faced. I submit that the danger to us as well is both great and real should we also fail to stand by Joseph.

Another who stood steadfast in the chilling wind of a contagious apostasy was Wilford Woodruff. He, like John Taylor, was called to replace those who had fallen, and he himself later succeeded President Taylor as the prophet. In discussing these matters and instruction given to him at the time of his call to the Twelve, he had the following to say:

He [meaning Joseph Smith] *taught us some very important principles, some of which I here name. . . . Brother Joseph laid before us the cause of those men's turning away from the commandments of God. He hoped we would learn wisdom by what we saw with the eye and heard with the ear, and that we would be able to discern the spirits of other men without being compelled to learn by sad experience. He then remarked that any man . . .*

who pursued a course whereby he would ignore or in other words refuse to obey any known law or commandment or duty—whenever a man did this, neglected any duty God required at his hand in attending meetings, filling missions, or obeying counsel, he laid a foundation to lead him to apostasy and this was the reason those men had fallen. [*JD* 21:190]

Note with care the risk attendant to violating commandments and covenants.

On another occasion, Brother Woodruff bore this testimony, which witness of Joseph and his mission was consistent throughout his life:

It has been my faith and belief from the time that I was made acquainted with the Gospel that no greater prophet than Joseph Smith ever lived on the face of the earth save Jesus Christ. He was raised up to stand at the head of this great dispensation—the greatest of all dispensations God has ever given to man. [*JD* 21:317]

This testimony was beautiful and clear, but what was even more impressive and helpful was the steady and stalwart behavior that Wilford Woodruff demonstrated in clearly and consistently standing by Joseph Smith.

Some of that original group of apostles and other followers seemed to have lost their testimonies, although Oliver and others apparently had not, in spite of their differences with Joseph. They just were not able to stand by Joseph when the heat and pressure became so severe.

What does it mean to us to stand by Joseph? We do not have a doctrine of infallibility. Joseph himself was quick to admit his own shortcomings, but he was also a very good and stable boy and man. In describing his own situation and occasional errors, he said: "No one need suppose me guilty of any great or malignant sins. A disposition to commit such was never in my nature" (JS—H 1:28). His openness on these matters was lifelong, and shortly before his death he said:

"I never told you I was perfect; but there is no error in the revelations which I have taught" (*Teachings*, 368).

Our testimonies are vital, but not sufficient by themselves. The Bible reminds us that even the devils believe in Jesus (see James 2:19). Our love and respect for Joseph Smith is important, but if it is not incorporated into our lives internally and consistently, we cannot stand by Joseph. We may not expect to have the same experiences that Oliver Cowdery and others had with Joseph Smith, but we can expect to have the same convictions—and to demonstrate them in the same way that Brigham Young, Heber C. Kimball, John Taylor, Wilford Woodruff, and countless more anonymous thousands have since the Restoration of the gospel.

Such conviction comes to us by study, by faith, and by always acting appropriately—and it is hard work. Those who I have named, as well as legions of others, have obtained this witness and internalized it through the manifestations of the Holy Ghost. The Holy Ghost is anxious to confer this sustaining knowledge to us because the testimony of Joseph's work and mission is key and central to our testimony of that which is most important of all: that Jesus is the Christ, our Savior and Redeemer, and the literal living Son of our living Heavenly Father.

How grateful we are to Joseph for his worthiness to witness what he did for us. How grateful we should be that we are allowed to "stand by" Joseph with our own actions and testimonies of the Father and the Son.

I have come to believe that this attitude is in large part the crux of the matter when the question of "Why BYU?" is asked. You know the account of our origins and our history. You know that our people, in their absolute poverty, have always sacrificed so that those who follow will have opportunities for excellent education in both things of the spirit and of the world. I hope you know that this is still the case. Although our collective circumstances are better than ever, we are still the beneficiaries of significant sacrifice on the part of many. Why should this be the case when the opportunities we enjoy are available to only a fraction of the worthy and desirous who wish to be where we are? I hope you are constantly thinking about this as I am.

Elder Neal A. Maxwell, in his last visit to BYU in the spring of 2004, shed some significant light on this matter. In his comments he included our excellent faculty and generous donors, as well as you special students, in his expressions of gratitude for what has been and is being accomplished here. Listen carefully to his words:

> *In a way LDS scholars at BYU and elsewhere are a little bit like the builders of the temple in Nauvoo, who worked with a trowel in one hand and a musket in the other. Today scholars building the temple of learning must also pause on occasion to defend the Kingdom. I personally think this is one of the reasons the Lord established and maintains this University. The dual role of builder and defender is unique and ongoing. I am grateful we have scholars today who can handle, as it were, both trowels and muskets.* ["Blending Research and Revelation," remarks at the BYU President's Leadership Council meeting, 19 March 2004]

We are here not only to achieve academically, not only spiritually, but also to do our parts in establishing the Church throughout the world and defending the kingdom. Happily, in our day we do not often actually use either trowels or muskets. We must, however, keep the metaphor in mind as we build our own knowledge while contributing as we can to the expansion of understanding in the world broadly. Likewise, we are here to strengthen faith and testimony, both personally and in the lives of those we are privileged to influence. In other words, we are here to do what Brigham Young and Gordon B. Hinckley expect us to do: to "stand by" Joseph.

We proclaim that the mission of Brigham Young University "is to assist individuals in their quest for perfection and eternal life" ("The Mission of Brigham Young University"). To this end, BYU seeks to develop students of faith, intellect, and character who have the skills and the desire to continue learning and to serve others throughout their lives. As has been stated repeatedly, these are the common aims of all education at BYU. We want everyone to achieve personally as much as is possible, but we do so with the important understanding that this goal is motivated by the desire to help each one of us be more effective in serving others.

Let me return to the counsel of the Lord to Oliver that provides the basis for my message today: "Therefore be diligent; stand by my servant Joseph, faithfully, in whatsoever difficult circumstances he may be for the word's sake" (D&C 6:18). In that context, Oliver Cowdery was given this additional counsel that I share with you now as you strive to incorporate into your own lives the necessary characteristics and determination that will allow you always and forever to stand by Joseph: "Be patient; be sober; be temperate; have patience, faith, hope and charity" (D&C 6:19). To these I would add also the necessity of the "mighty change" of heart (Alma 5:12–14) that gives one the perspective and conviction to stand by Joseph always—meaning being true constantly and consistently to the principles he taught and the Church that he established.

May we always be worthy and willing to "stand by my servant Joseph" is my prayer. In the name of Jesus Christ, amen.

Joseph Smith:
Lover of the Cause of Christ

———◆———

Heidi S. Swinton

The day was June 27, 1844. The place, Carthage, Illinois. In the early evening Willard Richards, a member of the Quorum of the Twelve Apostles, dispatched sobering news to the Saints in Nauvoo: "Joseph and Hyrum are dead. Taylor wounded, not very badly. I am well. . . . The job was done in an instant" (*HC* 6:621–22).

A cortege left the hostile county seat of Carthage early the next morning and arrived in Nauvoo just after three in the afternoon. The mourners were waiting in the streets for the return of their prophet-leader.

"My soul sickened and I wept before the Lord," William Hyde observed. "It seemed that the very heavens were clad in mourning" (William Hyde Journal, LDS Church Archives).

James Madison Fisher described the melancholy: "To see stout men and women standing around in group[s] crying and mourning . . . was enough to break the heart of a stone " (Aroet Hale, Reminiscences, LDS Church Archives).

———

Heidi S. Swinton, an award-winning author and screenwriter, was serving as a member of the Relief Society General Board when this devotional address was given at Brigham Young University on 2 November 2004. © Intellectual Reserve, Inc.

"The love the saints had for him was inexpressible," Mary Alice
Cannon Lambert lamented. "Oh, the mourning in the land!" (Mary
Alice Cannon Lambert in "Joseph Smith, the Prophet," *Young
Woman's Journal* 16, no. 12 (December 1905), 554).
These people had left homes, farms, and even families to gather
for the Word's sake. They saw themselves as saints; they saw Joseph
as a prophet called of God. For 14 years he had raised up this religion
on American soil. It was a religious movement that had attracted the
attention of the nation. Wrote Boston notable Josiah Quincy after an
1842 visit to the Mississippi river town of Nauvoo:

> *It is by no means improbable that some future textbook, for the use of
> generations yet unborn, will contain a question something like this: What
> historical American of the nineteenth century has exerted the most powerful
> influence upon the destinies of his countrymen? And it is by no means impos-
> sible that the answer to that interrogatory may be thus written:* Joseph
> Smith, the Mormon prophet. *And the reply, absurd as it doubtless seems
> to most men now living, may be an obvious commonplace to their descen-
> dants.* [Josiah Quincy, *Figures of the Past* (Boston: Little, Brown, and
> Company, 1926), 317; emphasis in original]

We are those descendants. Our lives, our very salvation, hinge on our
faith in the Lord Jesus Christ and in His gospel restored through the
Prophet Joseph Smith.
It isn't the life and history of this New Englander that spurs a
testimony. It is his words: "I had actually seen a light, and in the
midst of that light I saw two Personages, and they did in reality speak
to me" (JS—H 1:25). For years he stood all alone before the world
and testified of his vision in the Sacred Grove. He spoke with God
the Father and Jesus Christ face-to-face and shared what he had
learned with us. Joseph's testimony of the Savior, "that he lives!" is as
direct as it gets (D&C 76:22). Jesus Christ lives. Ponder on the significance of those words. Of his first vision of the Savior in the company
of our Father in Heaven, Joseph wrote, "I knew it, and I knew that
God knew it, and I could not deny it" (JS—H 1:25).

Years later, in Hiram, Ohio, he no longer stood alone. At his side was Sydney Rigdon as they "beheld the glory of the Son, on the right hand of the Father, and received of his fulness." Ponder on their words:

And now, after the many testimonies which have been given of him, this is the testimony, last of all, which we give of him: That he lives!

For we saw him, even on the right hand of God; and we heard the voice bearing record that he is the Only Begotten of the Father—

That by him, and through him, and of him, the worlds are and were created, and the inhabitants thereof are begotten sons and daughters unto God. [D&C 76:20, 22–24]

We are those sons and daughters.

Joseph was born to two good souls—Joseph and Lucy—in Sharon, a quiet little community in the hills of Vermont. The year 2005 is the 200th anniversary of his birth. His mother wrote, "We had a son whom we called Joseph after the name of his father; he was born December 23, 1805" (Lucy Mack Smith, *History of Joseph Smith by His Mother*, ed. Preston Nibley [Salt Lake City: Bookcraft, 1954], 46). His grandfather Asael had predicted that God would "raise up some branch" of the Smiths "to be a great benefit to mankind" ("Sketch of the Autobiography of George Albert Smith," *Millennial Star* 26, no. 27 [1 July 1865]: 407; also George A. Smith, "My Journal," *Instructor*, January 1946, 9; see also *HC* 2:443).

Joseph was that man.

That the Lord chose to restore His Church through a young man, not a graduate of an acclaimed school of religion or a preacher from one of the high pulpits in a well-established neighborhood, is unbelievable to those who measure in earthly terms. But this is not an earthly church, nor are we simply living out our days knowing only what is here and now.

John Taylor said:

Joseph Smith, the Prophet and Seer of the Lord, has done more, save Jesus only, for the salvation of men in this world, than any other man that ever lived in it. . . . He lived great, and he died great in the eyes of God and his people. [D&C 135:3]

Joseph was an uncommon man. Look at what he did. He translated the Book of Mormon by the power of God, received priesthood keys from ancient prophets, built temples, gathered the faithful to Zion, and taught doctrines that were given to him by direct revelation. The Lord said, "Whether by mine own voice or by the voice of my servants, it is the same" (D&C 1:38). When we hear Joseph speak, we hear divinity.

Joseph taught:

If you wish to go where God is, you must be like God . . . , for if we are not drawing towards God in principle, we are going from Him and drawing towards the devil. . . .

Search your hearts, and see if you are like God. [HC 4:588]

How would you answer that challenge: "Search your hearts, and see if you are like God"? Joseph's life was one of pure integrity to the cause of Christ, who he loved. He loved what the Lord loved. He lived the Lord's way. It wasn't easy for him. It isn't easy for us.

In 1829, while serving as Joseph's scribe, Oliver Cowdery asked for direction for his part in the unfolding gospel. In the revelation from the Lord that followed, Oliver was told succinctly: "Stand by my servant Joseph, faithfully, in whatsoever difficult circumstances he may be for the word's sake" (D&C 6:18). As with all references in the Doctrine and Covenants, He wasn't speaking to just Oliver. The Lord has made it clear, "I say unto you, that this is my voice unto all" (D&C 25:16).

"Stand by my servant Joseph." What does that mean for each one of us? Where do we stand when it comes to Joseph Smith and what he called "the cause of Christ" (HC 1:468)? After his martyrdom, as Joseph was returned to his people in a pine box, the streets of Nauvoo were lined with faithful members of The Church of Jesus Christ of Latter-day Saints. They honored him both in life and in death. It was a moment of truth in the Restoration. This was not Joseph's church; it was the Church of Jesus Christ. These faithful picked up their meager belongings buttressed by a faith that commanded their hearts, and they walked west to begin again. That's what it means to stand by Joseph. We stand as witnesses that Jesus Christ lives, and if we are called to unfamiliar ground, that's where we go. Our testimony is the treasure we take with us.

Lofty words? Not really. You are going to leave this "Nauvoo" of sorts here. Brigham Young University is a haven from the world. You have gathered from all countries to learn and to serve. That was the pattern in Nauvoo. Though the Saints never built the "University of Nauvoo," they were schooled just the same from God's chosen teacher, Joseph Smith. They learned that in spite of death, disappointment, difficulty, and setbacks, the gospel is true, Jesus Christ lives and directs His work, and eternal life is promised to all who believe and act in His name. Keep that perspective in mind as you leave here with your handcart or your wagon and go forth. Stand by Joseph as you work and raise your family. Don't be like Simonds Ryder, who turned from the truth because his name was spelled wrong on his missionary letter (see *HC* 1:260–61). Joseph was jailed more than 50 times for standing up for the Lord's word and His ways. What did he do when his jailers with coarse language and abhorrent behavior rabbled around outside his cell? As Parley P. Pratt recorded, Joseph stood and commanded: "Silence!"

Parley P. Pratt went on to describe:

Chained, and without a weapon; calm, unruffled and dignified as an angel, he looked upon the quailing guards, whose weapons were lowered or dropped to the ground. . . .

. . . I have tried to conceive of kings, of royal courts, of thrones and crowns; and of emperors assembled to decide the fate of kingdoms; but dignity and majesty have I seen but once, as it stood in chains, at midnight, in a

dungeon in an obscure village of Missouri. [*PPP,* 1985, 180; emphasis in original]

Will we be so valiant? Remember Joseph's words: "If we are not drawing towards God . . . , we are going from Him." Search your heart for your testimony of the Prophet. If yours is casual, seek for a spiritual witness of Joseph Smith's calling as a prophet for the latter days. That testimony is received not through books, tapes, or even talks—like this one—but by the Spirit confirming to your spirit that Joseph Smith was and is a prophet of God.

I received my witness not from study but from the Spirit when I was standing by a fence in Fayette, New York, outside the Peter Whitmer farmhouse. That ground is sacred to me, much like the mount for Moses—"for the place where thou standest is holy ground" (Acts 7:33). The Church was established there in 1830, in the middle of nowhere, as the world gauges place. There I received from the Spirit of God the confirmation "that Joseph was and is a prophet of God." I remember thinking at first, "I know that. Everybody knows that."

Then the words came a second time: "Joseph Smith was and is a prophet of God. Someday you will need to know that."

It was like the description in Jacob: "I had heard the voice of the Lord speaking unto me in very word . . . ; wherefore, I could not be shaken" (Jacob 7:5).

Someday is here for every one of us. The world needs our firm testimony of Joseph and the Restoration—right now.

Why did he stand upon his feet the morning after being tarred and feathered and preach the gospel of Jesus Christ with great conviction? Why did he endure a dark, lonesome prison—appealing to the Lord for comfort rather than shaking his fist at the sky for the unjust treatment? Why did he bury one child, then another and another and another, and continue to proclaim his undying devotion to the Lord and a love for His work? Why did he carry on when friends turned against him, when enemies attacked and killed the faithful, when the forces of the adversary raged all around him?

The answer is best described in his own words: "I am a lover of the cause of Christ and of virtue chastity and an upright steady course of conduct and a holy walk" (letter to William W. Phelps, 31 July 1832, in Joseph Smith, *The Personal Writings of Joseph Smith*, comp. Dean C. Jessee [Salt Lake City: Deseret Book, 1984], 246; original punctuation). His characterization of himself is so telling. "A lover of the cause of Christ" is such a simple way of describing what it means to take His name upon us and to love what He loves. When we stand by Joseph, from our perspective we see the world as "the cause of Christ." That changes things, doesn't it?

Joseph sent his closest allies to England to preach the word of God when he could have used them by his side in Kirtland. At that time apostasy was rampant in Kirtland. To engage in "the cause of Christ" we have to leave our comfort zone. We have to "go where you want me to go, dear Lord," as the song says (*Hymns*, 1985, 270). Sometimes it is a march to Zion's Camp with no battle at the end. Do we decry the calling with "What was that all about?" or do we trust in Him whose work this is? He knows the battlefields and where the battles are best fought and what the battles really are. It is fair to say, "We fight most battles in our own hearts." That's why love of "the cause of Christ" is so critical.

Joseph Smith was not a self-absorbed leader demanding fealty from his followers. This was a man of God who understood the proclamation of his leader, the Lord Jesus Christ: "I came by the will of the Father, and I do his will" (D&C 19:24). Do we? Joseph lived such commitment to his death. Such devotion wasn't easy then. It isn't easy today in a world that cycles daily around wants, material possessions, passions, pleasures, and personal gratification. There is no peace in that lifestyle, no happiness. No matter how much glory or goods we get from the world, they will never be enough because within us is the Spirit of God. The Spirit thrives on goodness and light. The Spirit loves what the Lord loves. The Spirit seeks peace and the promise of worlds without end.

Joseph understood distractions and did not squander "the time . . . to prepare to meet God" (Alma 34:32). He said, "Wherever

light shone, it stirred up darkness" (*HC* 6:51). Darkness fights for
place in this world; it stirs around in our lives. Hopefully we are not
among those "walking in darkness at noon-day" (D&C 95:6). Joseph
described his difficult times: "Deep water is what I am wont to swim
in" (D&C 127:2). He did not entertain the idea that he would sink.
He kept swimming. The Lord's comfort to Joseph in the dim cellar in
Liberty, Missouri, was this: "Know thou, my son, that all these things
shall give thee experience, and shall be for thy good" (D&C 122:7).
"Hold on thy way," the Lord told Joseph (D&C 122:9).

Are we holding on to that "way," the cause of Christ? Do we
define ourselves with the terms Joseph used—*virtue, chastity, holy
walk?* Or do clothes that are inappropriate, language that is not fit-
ting, or actions and choices that do not fit "a holy walk" camouflage
that cause?

Joseph's description of himself is a good example for us all. He
said, "All I can offer the world is a good heart and a good hand" (*HC*
5:498). Good hearts. Good hands. Isn't that the description of a true
disciple? Think of John the Baptist as he laid his hands upon Joseph
and conferred the Aaronic Priesthood. That significant event was followed weeks later by Peter, James, and John appearing to Joseph and
conferring the Melchizedek Priesthood by the laying on of hands. Do
we appreciate the majesty of the priesthood? Do we recognize that
worlds without number were created by that power?

I have sat in what we call the blessing chair at home and had
my husband lay his "good hands" upon my head and through the
power of the priesthood bless me with the desires of my heart. That
power has healed wounds; it has given me peace, direction, insight,
clarity, strength, and comfort. I am so grateful for the blessings of
the priesthood and its influence in our family. We raised all sons. We
were blessed with the best of boys who have become the best of men.
Their hands have rested on my head and blessed me by the power
of the priesthood. They have blessed others in Germany, England,
Belgium, France, and Australia with that same power. That, brothers
and sisters, is the cause of Christ.

The Lord said to the Saints in 1830, "Keep the commandments which you have received by the hand of my servant Joseph Smith, Jun., in my name" (D&C 19:13). What of forgiveness in a culture that seeks retribution, that sues for spilled drinks, that is in your face and on your case rather than offering mercy, patience, and encouragement to one who is struggling? And what of those times when we are feeling secure and successful? Do we pass by on the other side of those who are in need? What of courage to support another through the repentance process, courage to do the right thing, and courage to overcome addictions that can paralyze us in our progress home to our Heavenly Father?

Joseph's love of the Lord sustained him when the world was raging around him. He was even cheerful—cheerful because he really knew and believed the words of the Lord: "Be of good cheer, and do not fear, for I the Lord am with you, and will stand by you" (D&C 68:6). When we stand by Joseph, bearing witness of Jesus Christ, the Lord stands by us. He acts in our behalf. "I will go before your face," He has promised. "I will be on your right hand and on your left, and my Spirit shall be in your hearts, and mine angels round about you, to bear you up" (D&C 84:88).

The work of angels is often quiet or in secret. It is rarely of the magnitude heralded by the world. Sometimes we are those angels for others. Joseph learned that lesson in Harmony, Pennsylvania, when he was translating the gold plates. I have a favorite account from that period that speaks to my heart. It's about Joseph Knight, Sr., who gained a witness of the young Prophet in the earliest days of Joseph's ministry. He was the age of Joseph's father—an unlikely confidant or companion to the young Joseph.

One day Joseph Knight felt impressed to take some supplies to the Smiths down in Harmony, a quiet little community on the banks of the Susquehanna River. There in those waters just down the hill from their home, Joseph baptized Oliver and then Oliver baptized Joseph—the two having received the holy priesthood from John the Baptist. This is such a sacred place. There is still a spirit in the air—

and a few less pebbles on the bottom of the river, because I waded in to bring some home.

Busy translating the gold plates in the spring of 1829, Joseph had little time to farm or make a living. Knight, who lived across the border in New York, wrote in his journal:

> *I bought a barrel of mackerel and some lined paper for writing . . . nine or ten bushels of grain and five or six bushels* [of] *taters and a pound of tea, and I went down to see him and they were in want.* [Joseph Knight, Sr., Reminiscences (n.d.), LDS Church Archives, 6]

Imagine Knight standing in the country store rattling off what he needed and then pausing: "And give me some of that lined paper for writing. That will do it." Sandwiched between the mackerel and bushels of grain was "some lined paper for writing." Perhaps it is the writer in me that loves the image so much, but I don't think so. I think it's the lesson learned from an older man, the age of Joseph's father, hearing the prompting to take what was needed to a young— and even then controversial—Joseph Smith.

Picture Joseph Knight loading up his wagon with supplies. Joseph hadn't sent a fax or called on his cell phone. The Spirit had prompted Knight to do the work of angels. What does this say to all of us? When we dash out the door in the morning, do we load up our backpacks with our essentials and some to spare for someone else in need? Do we pray about how we can further "the cause of Christ" as we pursue our tasks? Do we listen for promptings through the day or have we dismissed the still small voice calling us to service because of our pressures, our schedules, or simply the lack of time available in our Palm Pilot–packaged life?

There is a wonderful scripture in Alma 29 that may help us keep our priorities straight and our ears ready to hear. Alma said:

> *I do not glory of myself, but I glory in that which the Lord hath commanded me; yea, and this is my glory, that perhaps I may be an instrument in the hands of God.* [Alma 29:9]

Joseph Knight was an instrument, an angel.

What about us? I remember when I was writing about Joseph Smith for national television. When I thought about what I was doing, I was paralyzed. I could just see meeting Joseph Smith in the next life and accounting for my efforts. All I wanted to do was to get it right—for him, the Prophet of this dispensation.

I had written a working script for the documentary being produced by Lee Groberg, and it was sent off for review by the sponsoring station in Vermont. The early response was heartening. "The first part is pretty good," the reviewer said. The script began with the Martyrdom and then backed up to place Joseph in the context of American religious history. Then the story focused on the unfolding of the Restoration through Joseph's life.

The reviewer's next statement was something like "When you get to New York . . . " And then she paused. I knew what she was going to say: ". . . all these angels start dropping down from the sky." She paused again and then said, "No one is going to believe you."

I listened.

"Take this Moroni."

I corrected her pronunciation, saying, "It's Mōrōnī."

"Oh," she said, "Mō-rō-nī. How are you going to show him? You aren't going to hook him up to wires and then fly him through the sky?"

I explained that the show would use images of where things happened, paintings depicting the setting, and stained-glass windows.

"I hate this part," she said, and then she hung up.

A few days later she called back: "I've got an idea. Why don't you show the gold plates? You could put one of your experts there next to the shiny little volumes, and he could point to them and talk about them. Then people would believe you, because they could see something."

"There's a problem with that," I said.

"I've thought about that," she responded. "You've probably got them encased in some special box because of their antiquity."

"No," I said, "that's not the problem. Joseph gave the plates back to Moroni, and he buried them or took them someplace else. Anyway, we don't have them."

Long pause. "I hate this part," she said, and slam went the phone.

She had yet to read the Kirtland section where we had angels on the roof of the temple in the middle of the day.

Tell the story of the Restoration without angels? No. Tell the story of Joseph without the tutoring of Moroni? Without Peter, James, and John? Not possible. We have been called to do our part, whether it is taking lined paper for writing or standing firm about the story of the Restoration. Where you will stand depends in great measure on your testimony of Joseph Smith.

At the death of his father, Joseph Smith said, "He was the first person who received my testimony after I had seen the angel, and exhorted me to be faithful and diligent to the message I had received" (*HC* 4:190).

Each of us has a part. Hyrum, his older brother, who received his own witness of Joseph and the work, said, "Joseph has the spirit and power of all the prophets" (*HC* 6:346).

Brigham Young's testimony of the Prophet is stirring: "I feel like shouting hallelujah, all the time, when I think that I ever knew Joseph Smith, the Prophet" (*JD* 3:51).

Where are your hallelujahs? Are they reserved for your GRE score or your next statistics quiz? For dreams of a job with a car allowance? For simply a car? Those things are important; I am not discounting doing the best we can do in our preparation for this life and a career. But those efforts are not why we are here, and they will not carry us where we want to go.

Joseph knew the struggles of making a living, the heartache of burying children, the weight of his ministry, and the tensions created by sharing and living what to his enemies was simply unbelievable. His influence with the Saints was extraordinary. The persecution they shouldered, the journeys they endured, the sacrifices they made, the fervor they manifested in support of what Joseph called "the king-dom of God on earth" (*Teachings*, 39) is without equal in latter-day religious history. Are we part of that legacy? Have we picked up the cause of Christ from them? Are we moving it forward? Will we find ourselves standing by Joseph?

Joseph taught, *"When the Lord commands, do it"* (*HC* 2:170; emphasis in original). Joseph Smith understood and exemplified that if we do what the Lord asks, "the cause of Christ" will move forward. Whether it's in the form of lined paper for writing, building a temple, or being that temple the Lord expects us to be, we each have a part. Yours is clear in the heavens. May it be clear in your hearts. Make next year the time for you to gain your own personal witness of Joseph Smith and live closer to the gospel he championed.

I bear my witness that Joseph Smith was and is a prophet of God. Gaining that testimony has changed my life. I would have stood to honor him as his body was brought back to Nauvoo. Where do you stand? Do you love the cause of Christ, and will you stand firm, no matter what difficulty you face, "for the word's sake" (D&C 6:18)? The word is the gospel. The Savior's gospel is the only way home to our Father in Heaven. I know that Jesus Christ lives, that my Redeemer lives, and that this is His work and His Church. And the glory be to the Father. In the name of Jesus Christ, amen.